Praise for
POINT MAN, REVISED AND UPDATED

"*Point Man* is a go-to resource for leading your family faithfully and well in the midst of an antagonistic culture. Steve Farrar calls on men not to simply do better but to be better. Jam-packed with biblical direction and leadership strategies, this battle guide will equip you to lead your family to victory."
—Dr. Tony Evans, president of the Urban Alternative and senior pastor of Oak Cliff Bible Fellowship

"Steve Farrar is a once-in-a-generation figure. His longevity as a truth-telling voice in a lie-believing world makes him uniquely trustworthy. *Point Man* is his signature work. Compressed on every page of this book you will find a hopeful, straight-shooting, tell-it-like-it-is, no double-talk prescription for men who are tired of reading spiritual pabulum. Steve will challenge and inspire you with the fervor of a prophet, the wisdom of a reformer, and the passion of someone who really cares."
—Patrick Morley, bestselling author, Bible teacher, and founder of Man in the Mirror

"*Point Man* is one of the most valuable books you will ever read. It had a huge impact on me decades ago and continues to today. Steve Farrar is a great, no-nonsense Bible teacher for whom I have the highest respect."
—Ken Harrison, chairman of Promise Keepers and CEO of WaterStone

"*Point Man* has rightly risen to the status of a classic. Like Caleb before him, Steve Farrar's strength, seasoned by decades of spiritual battle, is more acute and battle ready than ever before. The appendix is worth the price of the book. And chapter 5 will blow your mind—in a good way! Steve was a straight shooter back when. Still is. Fearless. Full of truth. Walks the talk. So strap in, rework your biblical masculine energy with Steve, and take the point."

—Stu Weber, pastor and author

POINT MAN

Revised and Updated

POINT MAN

Revised and Updated

HOW A MAN CAN LEAD HIS FAMILY

STEVE FARRAR

MULTNOMAH

Copyright © 2022 by The Estate of Steven James Farrar
Copyright © 1990, 2003 by Steve Farrar

All rights reserved.

Published in the United States by Multnomah, an imprint of Random House, a division of Penguin Random House LLC.

MULTNOMAH® and its mountain colophon are registered trademarks of Penguin Random House LLC.

Originally published in hardcover and in significantly different form in 1990, and subsequently in paperback in 1992 with a study guide, by Multnomah, an imprint of Random House, a division of Penguin Random House LLC. A first revised edition was published by Multnomah, an imprint of Random House, a division of Penguin Random House LLC, in 2003.

Library of Congress Cataloging-in-Publication Data
Names: Farrar, Steve, author.
Title: Point man : how a man can lead his family / Steve Farrar.
Description: Revised and updated. | Colorado Springs, CO : Multnomah, [2022] |
Includes bibliographical references.
Identifiers: LCCN 2021021864 | ISBN 9780525653523 (trade paperback) |
ISBN 9780593192733 (ebook)
Subjects: LCSH: Fathers—Religious life. | Parenting—Religious aspects—Christianity.
Classification: LCC BV4846 .F36 2021 | DDC 248.8/421—dc23
LC record available at https://lccn.loc.gov/2021021864.

Printed in the United States of America on acid-free paper

waterbrookmultnomah.com

6th Printing

Second Revised Edition

Interior book design by Diane Hobbing

SPECIAL SALES Most Multnomah books are available at special quantity discounts when purchased in bulk by corporations, organizations, and special-interest groups. Custom imprinting or excerpting can also be done to fit special needs. For information, please email specialmarketscms@penguinrandomhouse.com.

To James R. Farrar, my dad, in appreciation
for over sixty years of spiritual leadership
where it really counts. At home.

CONTENTS

1. Point Man on Patrol   3

2. Save the Boys   22

3. Real Men Don't   46

4. A One-Woman Kind of Man   69

5. Anorexic Men and Their Bulimic Cousins   94

6. Husband and Wife Teamwork in the Marriage Cockpit   114

7. Restoring the Ancient Boundaries of Gender and Marriage   138

8. How to Raise Masculine Sons and Feminine Daughters   163

9. Save the Girls   190

10. Telling Your Kids What You Don't Want to Tell Them   220

11. Start Your Own Nation   244

Appendix: The Meaning of Headship in the New Testament   259

Questions for Discussion and Reflection   265

Acknowledgments   273

Notes   277

POINT MAN

Revised and Updated

POINT MAN ON PATROL

It is harder to lead a family than to rule a nation.
—*Chinese proverb*

Albert Einstein was invited to speak at a banquet held in his honor at Swarthmore College. Hundreds of people from all over the country crowded an auditorium to hear what he had to say.

When it was time for him to speak, he stood up and told the astonished audience, "Ladies and gentlemen, I am very sorry, *but I have nothing to say.*" And he sat down. A few seconds later, he stood up again and said, "In case I have something to say, I will come back and say it." Six months later, he wired the president of the college with the message:

"Now I have something to say." Another dinner was held, and Einstein made a speech.[1]

Some thirty-five years ago, I spoke at a FamilyLife conference in Irvine, California. More than five hundred men filled the auditorium. My subject that morning was "Effective Male Leadership in the Home." I talked about the importance of being a committed husband and a tuned-in father. My time with those men was relatively brief—less than an hour.

When I finished my talk, both the usual and the unusual occurred. The usual thing was that several men made their way to the stage to talk with me. Some had questions, some had comments, and some just wanted clarification on a point. But then the unusual happened. The first man asked me a question that I had never been asked: "What have you written on this?" Then another man came up and asked me the same question. Then another walked up and asked the same thing. In the span of five minutes, fifteen men asked me the identical question. One right after the other.

That was unusual.

I had no answer for these men. Like Einstein, I had nothing to say. At least nothing that would fill a book.

But it started me thinking. Thereafter, whenever I spoke on the subject of effective male leadership in the home—whether in Phoenix, Boston, Dallas, Minneapolis, or Boise—I would get the same inquiry: "What have you written on this?" And my answer was always the same: "Nothing." But at some point I paused and said, "But if I ever do have something to say, I'll let you know."

I now have something to say.

This is a book for men. It's a book that talks about *how*

you can become an effective leader in your home. After many years of research and study, I've concluded that effective male leadership in American homes is going the way of the dinosaur. Some people are worried about the extinction of whales, condors, snail darters, or baby seals. Those are legitimate concerns. But let me shoot straight with you. I'm a lot more worried about the extinction of the men who know how to lead a family. And the effective male leader who knows how to lead his family is already on the endangered-species list.

Dr. James Dobson provided an insightful diagnosis: "The Western world stands at a great crossroads in its history. And it is my opinion that our very survival as a people will depend upon the presence or absence of masculine leadership in millions of homes. . . . I believe, with everything within me, that husbands hold the keys to the preservation of the family."[2]

Things have not gotten any better in the years since Dobson made that statement. If anything, the crisis has grown even more acute.

That's why I now have something to say. Three things, to be specific. And I want to say them to men—men who love their families, who care for their families, and who would die for their families.

WAR HAS BEEN DECLARED ON THE BIBLICAL FAMILY

You are only eighteen—in the absolute prime of youth. You've got a driver's license, a girlfriend, and plenty of dreams. Your entire life is ahead of you, but your immediate goal is to stay alive.

Welcome to Afghanistan.

On this particular day, you would give anything not to be here. Why? Because on this day you are going out on patrol. You've been on patrol before, but today is different, and that's why there's a knot in your gut and an icy fear in your heart.

Today is different because the patrol leader has appointed *you* to be "point man." In essence, you're the leader. Everyone else will fall in behind you. And as you move out to encounter the enemy, you realize that the survival of those seven men stepping cautiously behind you will depend on just one thing: *your ability to lead*. Your judgment may determine whether they live or die. The responsibility hangs over your head.

Your senses have never been so alive, your adrenaline so surging—you can almost hear it rushing through your veins. You know the enemy is near, maybe just hundreds of yards away. Intelligence reported heavy enemy activity in this area late last night. Your job is to confirm or deny that activity. For all you know, they're watching you right now. Perhaps they can see you, but you don't have a clue where they are.

As you gingerly make your way through the meadow thick with poppies, you've got one eye out for concealed wires in your path and another scanning the trees for snipers. Entire patrols have been lost because the point man failed to anticipate an ambush. Men have been killed or horribly maimed, all because a point lacked skill and wisdom.

You never saw it coming. The violent shock and utter surprise of gunfire momentarily paralyzes you, despite your "instant reaction" training. Before you can respond, a bullet tears through your flesh and explodes a bone in your leg. A thousand thoughts instantly flood your mind: *Am I going to die? Where are those shots coming from? Is there more than one? Will I lose my leg? Where's the patrol leader?*

One glance to your left tells you that the family of the patrol leader is now fatherless. In the chaos of attack, and in spite of your wounds, the other men are looking to you for direction. They know that you are the most experienced man. In panic situations like this, the book goes out the window. Like it or not, you are the leader.

As a medic evaluates your wound, you're trying to determine what to do next. *Just what is the situation? What are we up against? Where are they?* Some good news in the midst of confusion brings a ray of hope—the bleeding has stopped. You're luckier than most guys on point. Usually they're dead before they hit the ground. You're still alive and in control of your thinking.

Two other men beside the patrol leader were hit. One is dead, the other bleeding profusely. You get on the radio and report your situation and position. You request a chopper for the hemorrhaging private. But before you can finish your request, the hidden enemy unleashes all his firepower on your position. You're surrounded.

In your gut, you know the odds are against you. You're outnumbered, outgunned, and not in the greatest position to wage a counterattack. You've got two men dead, one dying, and four wondering if they'll make it to lunch. The worst-case scenario has happened . . . and it's worse than you ever imagined.

Now is the time your leadership will make the difference. What you say and do will determine whether your men live or die. As automatic weapons blaze around you, you must accurately assess the situation, determine the critical next steps, and formulate a flawless plan. It's leadership, pure and simple. If your plan works, you and half your men may get out alive. If it doesn't, someone will be lucky to find your dog tags.

Some reading this account don't have to use their imagination—you were actually there. You know what it is to see your buddy disappear forever behind the zipper of a body bag. You know firsthand the white-hot heat of phosphorous grenades and the adrenaline rush of a firefight. You know what it's like to be disoriented by the concussion of artillery shells crashing in around you. You don't have to imagine patrolling in Afghanistan . . . it's all you can do to get a night's sleep without reliving it again and again.

Let's make a critical change in the scenario. You're still in Afghanistan, on patrol in the same deceptively beautiful meadow. But something about this patrol is different. You're still the point man, but this time you're not leading a group of men.

You're leading your family.

You look over your shoulder to see your wife and children following behind. Your little girl is trying to choke back the tears, and your little boy is trying to act brave. Your wife is holding the baby and trying to keep him quiet. On this patrol, you don't want to engage the enemy; you want to avoid him.

What would you be feeling under such conditions? The survival of each member of your family—and its survival as a whole—would completely depend on your ability to lead through the maze of possible ambushes, hidden mines, invisible snipers, and all the extraordinary hazards of combat.

Would you be motivated? Would your senses and adrenaline be working overtime? Of course they would! You would know in your gut that the survival of your family was up to you. It's all on your shoulders . . . because you are the leader.

This is no imaginary situation. It is reality. If you are a husband or father, then you are in a war. War has been declared on the family—on your family and mine. *Leading a family through the chaos of American culture is like leading a small patrol through enemy-occupied territory.*

If you doubt such a war now rages in our country, take another look at the casualty list:

- Nearly one out of two marriages ends in divorce.[3]
- Tonight, enough teenagers to fill the Rose Bowl, Cotton Bowl, Sugar Bowl, Fiesta Bowl, and average Super Bowl will practice prostitution to support drug addictions.
- Back in 1960, most teen mothers were married; an estimated 15 percent of births to mothers ages fifteen to nineteen were to unmarried teens. Today, it has flipped: 89 percent of those in that age group who give birth are unmarried mothers.[4]
- Teens and young adults think it is more immoral not to recycle than to view porn.
- Almost two-thirds of teens and young adults have received images that are sexually explicit (usually from someone they are dating or a friend), and nearly half have sent such images.[5]
- The suicide rate for girls ages fifteen to nineteen doubled from 2007 to 2015, when the rate reached its highest point in forty years, according to the CDC. The suicide rate for boys ages fifteen to nineteen increased by 30 percent over the same time period.[6]

Let me ask you something: What are you doing to keep your marriage off the casualty list? You've seen divorce hit your friends and maybe even your extended family. Why won't it happen to you?

Then again, maybe it *has* happened to you. You know what it is to have your patrol ambushed. You never saw it coming, but as a result of the enemy's attack, you've lost your marriage and your family. You are still healing from that painful experience, even as you read these pages. I commend you and admire you for picking up this book.

Some of the most teachable people I meet are those who have endured the heartbreak of a divorce. Many of these men and women *never* want to repeat that experience. Because of their painful wounds, they soak up the truth of Scripture like thirsty sponges. This book will offer some principles to help you avoid another ambush in the future should you remarry. Or you may already have remarried and are dealing now with all the intricacies of leading a blended family. You are back on patrol. *Good man!*

Others are parenting solo—the toughest job in America. If that's you, I think you will find some encouraging words in these pages as well.

I applaud all you men who have been through a family ambush for taking the time to equip yourself for the ongoing battle against the enemy. God will honor your teachability.

I've asked how you intend to keep your marriage off the casualty list. Let me ask you something else: What are you doing to keep your *kids* off the casualty list? Not what is your wife doing, not what is the church youth-group leader doing, not what is the pastor doing, but what are *you* doing?

Because many of the kids on that casualty list are from Christian homes.

Maybe you have teenagers and don't have to be convinced there's a war going on. You see the casualties nearly every day. If you don't yet have teenagers, let me ask you another question: How long before your oldest kid hits thirteen? How much time do you have left? Two years? Five? Maybe ten?

Time is slipping through our fingers like spaghetti in the hands of a two-year-old. We must be actively working to prepare our children to defend themselves against the snipers, ambushes, and booby traps. This *is* war, and there are no guarantees our children will stay off the casualty list. But with God's help and our concerned leadership, we can greatly reduce the risks.

It's like the risk of a heart attack. None of us have any guarantees we won't suffer a cardiac arrest. Yet at the same time, it is also true that if a man quits smoking, watches his weight, participates in some type of aerobic exercise, and stays away from high-fat, high-cholesterol foods, he will greatly reduce his risk.

It's the same with our kids. There are no guarantees. You could do everything right, and your child could still rebel and pursue a life of drugs, promiscuity, and irresponsibility. Almost every kid will test the limits and rebel to some degree, actively or passively. Nevertheless, by consciously, constantly building moral strength into your child's life, you greatly reduce the risk of that happening in the teenage years.

War has been declared on the biblical family. But I have something else I want to say.

In Scripture, God gave us a blueprint for how the family is to function. The father is head of the family. Together with his wife, he raises his children in a home where Jesus Christ is the focus. The Bible is the most important book in the home. It is the responsibility of the parents, and ultimately that of the father, to make sure the children grow up in an environment that will enable them to one day become competent, responsible parents in their own right. This ensures the continuity of the biblical family for the next generation.

It is abundantly clear that the enemy wants to interrupt this link of biblical families from generation to generation. He does this by implementing two strategies:

Strategy #1: *To effectively alienate and sever a husband's relationship with his wife.* Such a division can be either physical or emotional. Both are equally effective.

Strategy #2: *To effectively alienate and sever a father's relationship with his children.* Again, such a division can be either physical or emotional. Both are equally effective.

Dave Johnson, a friend of mine who was a longtime policeman in San Jose, California, shared this story with me years ago. One morning, Dave was called to the scene of a family disturbance. When he arrived, he found another family that would soon be added to the casualty list:

> The woman was crying and yelling at her husband
> who was standing with his hands in the pockets of

greasy overalls. I noticed homemade tattoos on his arm, usually a sign that someone had been in prison. I was glad that my "fill unit" had arrived. I stepped from my patrol car. As I walked towards the two, I could hear the woman yelling at her husband to fix whatever he had done to the car so she could leave. He made no reply, but only laughed at her with a contemptuous laugh. She turned to me and asked me to make him fix the car. My fill unit broke in and we "split" the two up so that we could find a solution to the problem. I began talking to the husband who said that his wife was having an affair and she was leaving. I asked him if they had gone for counseling and he said that he was not interested.

He went on to say that he was interested in only getting his "things" back. He said that his wife had hidden them from him. I asked his wife about his things, and she said she wouldn't give them to him until she got one of the three VCRs they owned. I found out later that his "things" consisted of the narcotics he dealt in. The other officer went to the wife's car and began looking under the hood to see if he could spot the trouble. The husband walked over, took the coil from his pocket, and handed it to the officer. He then told his wife that she could have one of the VCRs if he could have his things. She finally agreed and went into the house. As she entered the house, I noticed two little girls standing in the doorway, watching the drama unfold. They were about eight and ten years old. Both wore dresses and clung to a Cabbage Patch doll. At their feet were two small suitcases. My eyes couldn't leave their faces as they watched the two people they loved most tear each other apart.

The woman emerged with the VCR in her arms and went to the car where she put it into the crowded back seat. She turned and told her husband where he could find his things. They both agreed that they had equal shares of the things they had accumulated in ten years of marriage. Then as I stood in unbelief, I watched the husband point to the two little girls and say to the wife, "Well, which one do you want?" Without any apparent emotion, the mother chose the older one. The girls looked at each other as the older one picked up her suitcase and then climbed into her mother's car. I had to stand and watch as the littlest girl, still clutching her Cabbage Patch doll in one hand and her suitcase in the other, watched her big sister and her mother drive off. I watched as tears streamed down her face in total bewilderment. The only "comfort" she received was an order from her father to go into the house as he turned to talk with some friends. There I stood, the unwilling witness to the death of a family.[7]

Families are dying all over America. They are dying on my street and on yours. And in every one of these dead homes, the autopsy would be the same. Cause of death: Strategy #1.

The enemy cannot kill a family without dividing the husband and wife, so that is where he puts his efforts. And it is working. It's a strategy that's been around for thousands of years. It's called divide and conquer.

But there's a flip side to the story. When a husband and wife refuse to allow anything to divide them, they become an impregnable force in the war on the family. When emotional energy is not spent on fighting each other, it can then be used *constructively* . . . to build the family.

When a husband and wife are committed to each other and to the Lord Jesus Christ, they can then begin to build their family on the solid foundation of the Word of God. Or to put it another way, they will build their home by teaching their children—and daily living out—a biblical worldview. A husband and wife who have a biblical worldview will take their counsel on life from the wisdom of God, not from the philosophy of men. When God's Word is our standard, it gives us and our children the compass of God's truth. This enables us to have God's perspective on right and wrong, which provides spiritual wisdom and discernment.

Researcher George Barna has done extensive studies demonstrating that fewer than 10 percent of self-proclaiming born-again Christians in the United States possess such a biblical worldview. The "10-percenters" are serious about their faith and committed to passing on the truth of God's Word to their kids. As a result, they make it a priority to not only spend time with their children but also teach them the Scriptures.[8]

To put it bluntly, you must decide to build your family and entire life on the Rock. Jesus and His Word are the foundation and rock of our lives. Those who obey Him are husbands and wives who are serious about their faith and committed to passing on the truth of God's Word to their sons and daughters—which will certainly have an impact on how these kids respond to life situations. The father, along with his wife's help, establishes an atmosphere in the home where anything and everything can be discussed with the kids. Every issue and situation, however, will be viewed through the lens of God's Word, not by popular opinion or the perspective of the world.

Barna's research indicates that the results of this approach can be significant. Here are a few positive statistics that demonstrate the wisdom of parents teaching their children a biblical worldview. Those children are

- 12 times less likely to engage in extramarital sex
- 9 times more likely to avoid adult-only material on the internet
- 5 times more likely to believe that Satan is real, not just a symbol of evil
- 5 times less likely to believe the Bible, the Koran, and the Book of Mormon are simply different expressions of the same truths
- 4 times more likely to reject the idea that a person can reach Heaven through personal goodness or doing good works[9]

By the way, teaching all these things takes time. Lots of time. You know the old debate about time, don't you? "Quality time" versus "quantity time." Some well-meaning parents who realize that their careers take too much time from the family choose to emphasize quality time. In their minds, their work is simply too demanding to have quantity time, so they make sure the time they do have with their families is quality.

That sounds good, but it has one fatal error: *you never know when quality time is going to show up.* Quality time isn't the norm. Quality time is when you can talk heart to heart with your kids. Quality time is when your son asks you a serious question completely out of left field as you are trimming the bushes together. Quality time is when you're putting your daughter to bed at night and she asks you to tell her a story about when you were a kid. It doesn't seem like any big deal at that moment, but it's a funny thing: she may remember it for the rest of her life.

Quality time usually makes an appearance someplace in the realm of quantity time.

Tom Peters is a prolific writer on the subject of business and excellence. He has either authored or coauthored such bestsellers as *In Search of Excellence, A Passion for Excellence,* and *Thriving on Chaos.* Listen to the words of this business guru who divides his time between homes in California and Vermont: "We are frequently asked if it is possible to 'have it all'—a full and satisfying personal life and a full and satisfying, hardworking professional one. Our answer is: No. The price of excellence is time, energy, attention and focus, at the very same time that energy, attention and focus could have gone toward enjoying your daughter's soccer game. Excellence is a high-cost item."[10]

High cost is right! It may cost you a child on the casualty list. It may cost you a son who turns to alcohol because Dad was never around. It may cost you a pregnant daughter who went to some adolescent male to meet her emotional needs because Dad was unavailable to fill her emotional tank.

Peters doesn't know it, but he's dispensing enemy propaganda. This successful writer is giving men permission to sacrifice their children on the altar of personal ambition. And he is wrong. Peters is to be commended for his honesty, but his reasoning is barbaric. An expert in marketing, he is marketing Strategy #2. And ultimately, Strategy #2 will eat your lunch. The enemy will use anything to alienate you from your children. Even a "passion for excellence."

You know, I have a passion to be an excellent father—and now a grandfather. I'm guessing you do, too, or you wouldn't have read this far. We need some men who have a passion to be better fathers than they are accountants. We need some men who have a passion to be better dads than they are attorneys, salesmen, foremen, pastors, or doctors.

Are you one of these men? You can be!

So far in these opening pages, I've said two things—but they may be among the most important things you've heard in a long time: (1) War has been declared on the biblical family, and (2) Satan's two specific strategies in this war are to alienate you from your wife and to alienate you from your kids.

But I have something else I want to say.

SATAN'S STRATEGY IN THE WAR
ON THE FAMILY IS TO NEUTRALIZE THE MAN

Baseball's legendary manager Leo Durocher was coaching first base in an exhibition game between the old New York Giants and the cadets at West Point.

> One noisy cadet kept shouting at Leo, doing his best to upset him.
>
> "Hey, Durocher," he hollered. "How did a little squirt like you get into the major leagues?"
>
> "My congressman appointed me," Leo shouted back.[11]

Not only is that a great comeback, but it also reveals how you got to be head of your family: you were appointed. Like it or not, you carry the responsibility. You are the point man.

The enemy is no fool. He has a strategically designed game plan, a diabolical method he employs time and time again. When he wants to destroy a family, he focuses on the man. If he can neutralize the man, he has neutralized the family. And the resulting damage is beyond calculation.

Satan's approach is the same, whether he's doing combat in the church or in the family. If he can neutralize a pastor through the man's financial impropriety or sexual escapade, he has neutralized that pastor's church as well. Not only has the pastor's reputation been tarnished, but the church's has as well, possibly for a generation. Satan's strategy has always been to neutralize the leaders.

That means we should *expect* to be attacked. We should *expect* extreme temptation to come our way. When you get serious about leading your family, you will be opposed.

If a man is passive and indifferent to the things of God and the spiritual leadership of his home, then attack isn't necessary. He's already neutralized. But the moment a man gets serious about following hard after Christ, he can expect the shelling to start. The enemy wants you neutralized, and he is not pleased when you begin to give spiritual leadership to your wife and children.

May I ask a question? What do you suppose Jesus Christ thinks about the failure of men to assume their God-appointed leadership roles? Jesus Christ established the family. Jesus Christ was incarnated into a family. He had brothers, sisters, and a genealogy. Perhaps the Lord would look at our contemporary situation and modify something He said at another time, in another culture. Perhaps He would say something like this:

> When He saw the leaders, He was filled with dismay, because so many quit, so many were set aside, and so many were plateaued and directionless. They had lost their zest for leading. They had *no clear philosophy or direction for their leadership. They were leaderless leaders. Then He said to His disciples, "The harvest is plentiful, but the leaders with clear direction are few. Ask the* LORD *of the harvest, that He will send forth knowledgeable, discerning, and direction-oriented leader-laborers into His harvest."*[12]

In the war on the family, the harvest is our children. They are the leaders and the parents of the next generation.

What will turn the tide in the war on the family? In the months prior to the last presidential election, I heard many evangelicals talk about the necessity of electing a Christian president. "Wouldn't it be great to have a committed Christian in the White House?" they asked. I would like to suggest something else that, in my opinion, would have far greater impact. If hundreds of thousands of men seriously began to lead in their own homes, the impact on America would be far greater than one Christian man leading in the White House.

It is estimated that when Canada geese fly in formation, they can fly 70 percent farther than when they travel alone.[13] If Christian men all over America would get into battle formation and begin to lead, we could turn this war around—and we could turn it quickly.

That's what I wanted to say.

I know that you love your family. You love your wife. You love your children. You would be willing to die for them. In most wars, that's what men are asked to do. They go off to war because they're willing to die for their families.

But in this war, it's different. In this war, Jesus Christ is looking for men who will *live* for their families. That's what He would have you do.

In the spiritual war on the family, it is the father who leads best.

2

SAVE THE BOYS

A boy is the only thing that God can use to make a man.
—*Cal Farley*

Thirty years ago, *Washington Post* columnist William Raspberry wrote these prescient words that still stand true today: "If I could offer a single prescription for the survival of America . . . it would be: restore the family. And if you asked me how to do it, my answer—doubtlessly oversimplified—would be: save the boys."[1]

Richard John Neuhaus shot straight about our present state of affairs: "Millions of children do not know, and will never know, what it means to have a father. More poignantly, they do not know anyone who has a father or is a father."[2]

Read that last sentence again, slowly. It staggers the imagination.

Each fatherless generation has given rise to another until

we now find ourselves in an almost inconceivable place. When a boy has no father, he will be clueless about fatherhood. The stunning result is that the young men of our day have largely become a generation of lost boys.

The enemy has effectively removed fathers from their God-appointed positions of leadership and responsibility by aiming at one simple goal: *destroy the boys by neutralizing the fathers.*

Fatherlessness, by the way, comes in many forms. It is not just physical absence or abandonment. It can come in the form of narcissistic bullying and abuse. Or it can come in the far-less-noticed form of relational detachment and emotional distance. All is fatherlessness.

Economics and ethnicity have little to do with it. A lost boy can grow up in wealth and affluence, going to the best schools and having every opportunity in life, just as easily as he can grow up in the inner city. But we know this: wherever fatherlessness prevails, anger and hopelessness become the predominant emotions among our boys, and with fatherlessness comes a correlating higher rate of crime and drug addiction, lower performance in schools, lesser ability to keep a job, and an explosion of out-of-wedlock births. Facts are stubborn things, and the facts bear this out.

But I don't have to convince you of this. You've seen it playing out before your eyes.

I recently heard it said this way:

> No culture will ever rise above the character of its men: fathers. . . . The only hope for stability and the only hope for sanity, the only hope for peace in a society is masculine, virtuous men. . . . Oh, there are lots of men at the gym, pretty buff, have some mus-

cles, but they're doing virtually nothing to stop the tide of evil in the world. . . . Weak, immoral men abuse women, and they produce more weak, immoral sons. . . . We are in some serious trouble because the current crop of men are infecting the children. . . . Weak men produce the death of society. . . . Something has to break the cycle.[3]

I'm an optimist, but the magnitude of this catastrophe overwhelms my ability to comprehend it. America is in crisis because men are no longer strong and virtuous influences in the lives of their boys. How long can a nation survive such a pattern? We are like a bullet train racing blindly toward a precipice from which there is no point of return.

No, William Raspberry did not oversimplify the solution: we must save the boys. I must save my boys, and you must save yours. If our boys are not equipped to lead virtuous, godly lives, then their children will be affected and the vicious cycle of fatherlessness will multiply with each successive generation.

If you don't have boys, then your energy should go into saving your girls. I know because I have a very special daughter. Little boys and little girls must both be saved if the family of the next generation is going to have any kind of fighting chance. So whether it's all boys in your home or all girls or a mixture of both, it's your job to provide a model that will equip them to confidently take on the responsibilities of life and marriage. That's why I'm devoting a section of this book to the important role of a dad in his daughter's life.

But if you have a son, you are the central person in his life. You hold the key that unlocks the mystery of manhood for him. Just as you looked to your dad, your son looks to you above any other man. He does not need you to be perfect. He just needs to know you care enough to be focused, intentional, and present. And he needs you to admit your mistakes when you make them. Your son will love and respect you all the more for that. Above any other man, you are the one who can help him discover his strengths and teach him how to be a man.

Let's face it. If our nation is to survive, the buck stops with men—and their boys. That's why the immediate task before us is to save our sons. They will be the fathers and leaders of the next generation. It's up to fathers to break the cycle of wickedness in a society.

So, how does a father save his boys?

THE ETERNAL PLAN FOR SAVING THE BOYS

From eternity, God instituted a plan for dads. It was to be followed by each generation. And for thousands of years, it was followed. His plan was given to us through Moses some three thousand years ago:

> You shall love the LORD your God with all your heart and with all your soul and with all your might. These words, which I am commanding you today, shall be on your heart. *You shall teach them diligently to your sons and shall talk of them when you sit in your house and when you walk by the way and when you lie down and when you rise up.* (Deuteronomy 6:5–7)

Fathers are to teach their sons diligently and continually. *Diligence* carries the idea of being persistent, hardworking, mindful, and attentive. *Continually* implies a constant, habitual way of life: when you are at home, when you go through your day, when you go to sleep, and when you rise up.

Dave Simmons, creator of "Dad the Family Shepherd" seminars, was correct: "*The task of a father is not to raise children: it is to equip child-raisers.*"[4] You are the mentor, the instructor, the shepherd of your sons so that they can shepherd the next generation of men.

That's God's eternal plan. But it can happen only if you are there.

THE FIRST PRINCIPLE OF FATHERING: *BEING THERE*

Error increases with distance. In my estimation, that's the basis of the first principle of fathering: if you are going to save the boys, you must start by *being there.*

I am an excellent bowler. I carry an average of 285. The goal of any bowler is a 300 game. Over the years, I have rolled nearly twenty 300 games. But there's something I should mention. The length of a bowling alley is approximately sixty feet. I, however, prefer to bowl from about fifteen feet.

When I bowl from fifteen feet, I enjoy the game a lot more. The majority of my balls are strikes, and when I do leave a spare, I always make it. I'm dynamite from fifteen feet. But when I move back to the regulation line, my average drops dramatically. The reason is simple: error increases with distance.

What is true in bowling is true in fathering. Error increases with distance. In other words, if I am going to be the family leader God has called me to be, then *I must be there.* On-site. Consistently.

Samuel Osherson wrote, "What does it mean to be male? If the father is not there to provide a confident, rich model of manhood, then the boy is left in a vulnerable position."[5]

We save our boys by *being there.* Being present, available, focused, and involved. A little boy naturally looks to his dad for cues. But if Dad isn't around, where will he look?

This raises a huge question: How can a father who truly cares about his sons "be there" when he can't "be there"? Most of us have jobs and responsibilities that remove us from our boys during almost all their prime waking hours. Would God command a father to do something he cannot do? The answer is no. Our Father never asks the impossible of His men. He always provides a way. But He wants us to use our heads and our hearts.

We've got to think like soldiers in battle. Before we can wrestle this issue to the ground, we've got to understand the forces we're up against, forces in play today that have changed fathering profoundly.

The Revolution of Fatherhood

For most of human history, fathers were *with* their sons from morning until night.

Think about that. It meant there was tremendous stability in the family. Boys grew up learning how to be men because they had seen models. They were prepared for the responsibilities of adulthood because their dads had prepared them. Boys watched their dads in action and received hands-on training until they launched into adulthood themselves. It's hard for us to grasp the normal pattern of family life that existed for centuries upon centuries.

But somewhere along the way, we lost our ability to "be there." How did we lose it?

The answer comes in three words: the Industrial Revolution. Not the sexual revolution or the Revolutionary War but the good old Industrial Revolution that we studied back in school.

You probably recall how, in that classic movie *Back to the Future,* actor Michael J. Fox got into a wild time machine (a souped-up DeLorean) and went back to the 1950s. It's been a while since we've reviewed our grade school notes on the Industrial Revolution. So let's use our imaginations, get into our own DeLoreans, and go back to the year AD 1750.

I dusted off the pages of our family's *World Book Encyclopedia* for some insight:

> In 1750, farming was the most important occupation. . . . The ordinary man was a farmer and lived in a village. He raised his own food, and unless he was near a large town he grew little more than he needed. Cloth and clothing, furniture, and tools and implements were made at home from wool, wood, and leather produced on the farm. The ordinary man bought little outside his village except iron for his plow point, salt, and perhaps an occasional ornament or bit of ribbon.
>
> In the towns, which were generally quite small, some manufacturing was carried on. Such things as hardware, cloth, jewelry, silverware, swords, guns, cannons, and ammunition were produced by craftsmen working in their own shops with simple tools.[6]

Men worked at home, women worked at home, and so did the children. Their jobs were different, but everyone worked. Moms nurtured the children until they were somewhere between five and seven, and then the boys would work alongside their fathers, and the girls would work alongside their mothers.

This had been the pattern of life for centuries.

Four out of five Americans were farmers. Those men who weren't farmers were silversmiths, blacksmiths, other types of "smiths," or various merchants. But the same basic pattern applied to them. When a boy reached seven, he would go to work with his dad and learn his trade. Going to work simply meant going from one room to another: "In many cases, [they] used their front rooms as workshops and sales rooms and lived in the back rooms."[7] If a boy wished to learn a new trade, his dad oversaw that as well. He searched for a man of good reputation and skill, and when his son was old enough, he took him to work under that man's tutelage as an apprentice or journeyman.

The normal pattern of life was for fathers to oversee their sons' entire training and development until manhood. For most dads, this meant being with their sons nearly every waking hour. Boys learned how to endure through hardship; they developed a strong work ethic and confidence so that when the time came, they would possess the wherewithal to take on the responsibility of leading and providing for their own families. They welcomed that time. They learned to deal with disappointment, take initiative, and be courageous in the face of danger, for difficulty and danger were always around the corner.

Then came the Industrial Revolution.

In the late 1700s to early 1800s, factories sprang up in cities everywhere. And that one change rocked our world. Soon enough, a man could no longer expect to be successful as an independent producer. To make a living, he had to leave home and go work in a factory, often for very long hours.

"Factory towns grew rapidly, and *serious social evils developed*."[8] Doesn't that comment—"serious social evils developed"—just drip with understatement? Author Weldon Hardenbrook explained:

> This dramatic transition literally jolted the role of men in America. Once farmers, and the children of farmers, these men exchanged work around their homes and families for new occupations in factories. And in most cases, this new situation required men to leave their homes for long periods of time.[9]

The removal of dads from the home meant the removal of a father's hands-on relationship with his sons. Dads could no longer shape and prepare them as a way of life.

The formula was simple:

Less Time = Less Influence

You can see why it became increasingly harder to save the boys.

Almost overnight, men stopped doing what they had done for thousands of years. They unknowingly brought to a halt the accumulated momentum of generations. Work now separated father from son. Men stopped raising their boys because they weren't present to lead them. And as the years went by, that all-important male role model eroded even further.

Who took up the mantle of raising our boys? By necessity, it was mothers—strong, intelligent, and resourceful mothers. They poured their hearts into teaching, disciplining, and building character into them. As the decades rolled by, a young boy's world became increasingly surrounded by women: grandmothers, teachers, extended family and sitters, and, most important, moms. We thank God for these women.

Many godly women influenced my life in my growing-up years, not the least of which was my remarkable mom. All my friends wished they could have her as their mom. They still do, as a matter of fact! My life would not be what it is today without her mark on my life. She loved me, prayed for me, encouraged me, oversaw my education, talked with me any time of the day or night, and disciplined me when necessary—which was fairly often. *Yet as valuable as she was to me, God never intended for her to teach me how to be a man. It was my dad who taught me how to be a man.*

How does a boy learn how to be a man? He learns it from another man.

But what happens when there isn't a man to teach him?

The Feminization of Men

I grew up in the sixties. Perhaps you or your father did too. In 1966, Dr. Marion Levy made this stunning observation:

> Our young are the first people of whom the following can be said: *if they are males, they and their fathers and their brothers and sons and all the males*

they know are overwhelmingly likely to have been reared under the direct domination and supervision of females from birth to maturity. . . . After all, *this has never held true of any substantial proportion of any population for even one generation in the history of the world before the last fifty years. . . .* But most of those living today will live to see what this will be like![10]

You and I are living in that day, and we are seeing what it is like.

When a boy is taught by women and surrounded by them for most of his waking hours, it is natural that he will internally adopt the outlook and reactions of those women. Why would he not? Without realizing it, he will become "feminized."

Let me make something clear. Feminization has nothing to do with effeminacy or homosexuality. Feminization is an internalized viewpoint, a way of thinking and reacting that is subconsciously more feminine than masculine. An all-star professional football player can be feminized. A president of the United States can be feminized. A champion Iditarod musher can be feminized. A powerful, well-spoken pastor can be feminized.

Dr. Stephen Clark, in his monumental book *Man and Woman in Christ,* gives the best definition of feminization I've ever come across. I urge you to read it carefully and with an open mind:

> A feminized male is a male who has learned to behave or react [in ways] that are more appropriate to women. The feminized male can be normal as a

male, with no tendencies to reject being male and no tendencies toward homosexuality, and yet he can have been so influenced by women or can have so identified himself with a world in which women dominate, that many of his interests and traits are more womanly than manly. Compared to men who have not been feminized, he will place *much higher emphasis and attention on how he feels and how other people feel.* He will be much more gentle and *handle situations in a "soft" way.* He will be much *more subject to the approval of the group,* especially emotionally expressed approval (that is, how others feel about him and what he is doing, how others react to him). He will sometimes tend to relate by preference to women and other feminized or effeminate men, and will sometimes have a difficult time with an all-male group. He will *tend to fear women's emotions,* and in his family and at work he can be easily controlled by the possibility of women (his mother, wife, or co-worker) having an emotional reaction. He will tend to idealize women and, if he is religious, he will tend to see in women the ideal Christians or the definition of what it means to be spiritual. *He will identify Christian virtue with feminine characteristics.*[11]

Don't be shocked if you see something of yourself here. The first time I read Clark's definition, I realized that some of it described me. I was shocked because I had a father who spent lots of time with me. But even with a connected father, you can still catch the virus of feminization, and no face mask can protect you from its unseen influence.

There is nothing wrong with a tender spirit of kindness, or an ease in recognizing and expressing emotions, or keen awareness and sensitivity to the feelings of others. These are human and godly traits. But there is everything wrong with a man who is primarily driven by these traits to the detriment of his deeper call to manliness. If we look at the ultimate man, the Lord Jesus, we see that He could be tender when it was appropriate, and He could be tough. When it came to the Pharisees, He was tough and aggressive, because that was the appropriate action that needed to be taken.

These days, feminization is in the air that we breathe. You cannot entirely prevent it from seeping into your life in some way. But here's the good news, and you need to hear this loud and clear:

- Feminization can be detected.
- Feminization can be avoided.
- Feminization can be reversed.

How is feminization reversed in a boy or man? By him spending time around strong and virtuous men. Look for men who are unafraid to speak truth and take on hard things. Men who instinctively fight evil and intercede for the weak and defenseless. Men who have integrity and do not compromise. Men who possess a balance of kindness and fortitude. Men who act like men.

I've seen dads reverse feminization in their sons by simply spending more time with them. That's actually the key. Two hours a week of focused time and activity with Dad can change a boy in a matter of months. But don't stop after a few months. You have to keep it going. He needs to be with you. He needs to be with his grandfather. Boys need to be around mature men. That's how you reverse feminization. Boys need to be with men who have godly character and model it in their behavior.

THE SECOND PRINCIPLE OF FATHERING:
TEACHING THEM TO ACT LIKE MEN

Part of saving our boys means teaching them how to *act like men.*

This is also part of the eternal plan of God for fathers: as you go, teach your sons how to act like men. It permeates the pages of Scripture. For example, David said to his son Solomon, "Show yourself a man" (1 Kings 2:2, NIV). And don't miss this: you are to do it in love. You're not a drill sergeant; you're a dad.

Wrapping up his first letter to the church at Corinth, the apostle Paul wrote these inspired words: "Be on the alert, stand firm in the faith, *act like men,* be strong. Let all that you do be done in love" (1 Corinthians 16:13–14).

The phrase "act like men" has to do with *courage* and *fortitude.* What does it mean to act like a man? It means to have fortitude, courage, willingness to risk, and an uncompromising faith in the living God. And to *do it all in love.*

You'll never find a better example than that of Jesus, the God-Man. Jesus possessed the perfect balance. He knew how to bring each trait of godly manhood to bear—at just the right time, in just the right way. There wasn't a feminized bone in His body. He healed the sick and wept with those who sorrowed, but He also turned over the tables in the temple. He loved the little children but cursed any man who would cause one of those little ones to stumble. He forgave the woman caught in adultery, but when it became necessary, He spoke truth to the Jewish leaders, calling them sons of Satan and children of that murderer and father of lies (see John 8:44). He had incredible courage and fortitude in the face of death, but "greater love has no one than this, that he lay down his life for his friends" (John 15:13, NIV). Truly He was the ultimate man.

That is the image of manhood we must teach our boys.

Canceling Manhood

You may have noticed that masculinity is not real popular these days.

In the past thirty years, manhood and masculinity have come under something akin to nuclear attack. That should not be surprising, because God loves men, He created men, and He's for manhood and masculinity. In our times, you can pretty much figure that if God is for something, the culture will be against it.

Modern-day men have undergone a national identity crisis. While women have risen higher and higher, men have felt increasingly overwhelmed, overpowered, and unable to fight against the trend. They have felt "canceled." It's a disastrous state of affairs.

By the way, may I be so bold as to ask this question? Who is now raising our boys? That's a question every Christian man and woman has to be willing to ask. With both parents in full-time careers, who is inculcating their sons with a love for the Lord and His words? Who is consistently building their character? Who is overseeing their friends and education? Who is watching closely for signs of deep insecurity, depression, crisis, confusion, or addiction?

The cards are stacked against our sons by this sheer fact: they are living in a culture that thinks very little of strong masculinity. Our boys are breathing in the air of a toxic, aggressively feminist cancel culture. The world they walk into every day is openly hostile toward real manliness and God-designed male leadership. That's why you have to be in your son's life, affirming his masculine DNA and coaching him through the tangled complexities of such an upside-down world.

Be encouraged by this: boys innately aspire to be men. We cannot let that innate desire be snuffed out before it is allowed to flicker into an unquenchable flame. A well-coached boy has a fighting chance to defy the odds and become a secure and strong man, balanced, virtuous, and at ease in his masculinity.

That is how the tide of a culture is turned, one boy at a time.

Putting a New Link in the Chain

Author James Carroll observed that "the curse of fatherhood is distance, and good fathers spend their lives trying to overcome it."[12] We may have had fathers who were absent from us, but we need not pass that on to our children. We must put a new link in the chain, a positive to replace a negative. If you do that, your boys will never have to deal with the emotional wounds that you may carry.

We save our boys by giving them role models to follow. When our boys have clear role models, they intuitively know how to function when they assume the responsibility of marriage and parenting. But in this generation, there are too many crippled boys who have no idea what it is to be a man.

It was my God-appointed task to ensure that my sons would be ready to lead a family. I had to equip them to that end. Little boys are the hope of the next generation. They are the fathers of tomorrow. They must know who they are and what they are to do. They must see their role models in action. That's how they will know what it means to be a male. That put the ball in my court . . . and puts it in yours.

I have three children. When my daughter, Rachel, was ten years old, her primary role model was her mother. Generally speaking, the girls emulate their mother and the boys follow after Dad. Guys, let's face it. Most of our wives are doing excellent jobs in getting our daughters ready for adulthood. Later in this book, I will deal specifically with a man's responsibility to his daughter. But for right now, I am going to assume your wife is carrying out her responsibility well in training your daughter.

This is a book for men. It's our job to save the boys. So the question is, How are we going to do that?

When my boys, John and Josh, were eight and five, I had a pretty clear idea of what I needed to teach them before they headed off to college. I remember asking myself, *What do I specifically need to do to train them to become leaders of their families?* I had five goals for saving my boys. It was (and still is) my job as their father to model for them the importance of the following:

- knowing and obeying Jesus Christ
- knowing and displaying godly character
- knowing and loving my wife

- knowing and loving my children
- knowing my gifts and abilities so I can work hard and effectively in an area of strength rather than weakness, contribute effectively to the lives of others, and have a little fun at the same time

You want something to pray for every morning when you arise? Pray for your boys, fervently and specifically. Pray for their future wives. Pray that they will find their niche in life. Pray that they will come to know Christ.

Will you make mistakes? Every guy has a handicap in the game of fathering.

I certainly do. I've made lots of mistakes along the way, and I imagine you will too. I can't recount to you all the times I've missed it with my boys. But God is merciful. And I can tell you from experience that humility with your sons goes a very long way. Our boys need us to be approachable and human. But they also need us to stay in the good fight for their manhood.

Not long ago, three military recruiters accepted an invitation to address the senior class of a local high school. Graduation was only a few months away, and the principal wanted his two hundred young men to hear about the options available in the military.

The assembly was to be forty-five minutes in length. It was agreed that each recruiter would have fifteen minutes to make his pitch and then have another twenty minutes in the cafeteria to meet with interested boys. The Army recruiter went first and got so excited about his speech that he went over twenty minutes. The Navy recruiter, not to be outdone, stood up and also spoke for twenty minutes.

The Marine Corps recruiter, realizing that his fifteen-minute speech had been cut to two minutes, walked up to the podium and spent the first sixty seconds in silence. Wordlessly, he gazed over the group of high school seniors. They knew he was sizing them up. After what seemed to be an eternity, the recruiter said, "I doubt whether there are two or three of you in this room who could cut it as marines. I want to see those three men as soon as this assembly is dismissed." He was mobbed by a herd of young men when he arrived in the cafeteria.

The Marine Corps is always on the lookout for a few good men. So is the Lord. As a matter of fact, He wants you. And with His help, you can make a difference in this war.

One man *can* make a difference. Churchill saved England. Belichick turned the Patriots from average into legends, and the ageless Brady quarterbacked them into six Super Bowl wins. Steve Jobs returned to Apple when they were on life support, and the rest is history. It happens all the time. One man can make a difference.

If you were to get into your DeLorean and travel into the future, what would your legacy look like? Would there be a chain, linking generation to generation with godly men who in turn produced more godly men? Or is it going to be generation after generation of confused leadership from men who have no clear-cut role models?

You are to teach your sons as you are *with* them. If you're not with them, you can't teach the truth of God. So you've got to make sure you have time for them. Jesus modeled this with His disciples. He was with them, and when He was with them, He was teaching them.

I know that you probably have a full-time job, but you can see the importance of not making a god out of your career. You've got to have time to be with your kids—to go through life with them and talk with them. This is the model for dads to follow.

This is where we have a real disadvantage compared with the pre–Industrial Revolution generation. We get up in the morning and leave for work. Our kids get up and go to school, and we probably won't see them until dinner. We've lost a significant amount of time with our sons because the demands of our culture have taken the time away.

In our world, fathering requires being proactive and creative. It takes energy and thought. It means moving toward your son intentionally and purposefully. It means putting your phone away and turning off the computer. It means playing with him when you'd rather be doing something else. It means spending one-on-one time you'd rather spend on yourself. It means getting to know your son—what he's afraid of, what he loves.

You are looking for quality moments, those teaching moments when doors open up in conversations or activities and your son is suddenly totally tuned in and tracking with you. When that happens, you walk right through those teachable openings and "seize the moment."

As we saw in chapter 1, there is a myth that you can plan quality time or make it happen on your own terms. The truth is that *quality* time happens in the midst of *quantity* time. You can't put it on a calendar. You can't just make it happen. It shows up during the everyday activities of life. This means that the more quantity time you spend, the greater the chances of those quality moments showing up.

For some men, it will mean saying no to a job that pays more because it will prevent you from being there. For others, it will mean leaving work to be present for important events in your son's life.

One man who didn't use the time wisely tells his story:

I remember talking to my friend a number of years ago about our children. Mine were 5 and 7 then, just the ages when their daddy means everything to them. I wished that I could have spent more time with my kids, but I was too busy working. After all, I wanted to give them all the things I never had when I was growing up.

I loved the idea of coming home and having them sit on my lap and tell me about their day. Unfortunately, most days I came home so late that I was only able to kiss them good night after they had gone to sleep.

It is amazing how fast kids grow. Before I knew it, they were 9 and 11. I missed seeing them in school plays. Everyone said they were terrific, but the plays always seemed to go on when I was traveling for business or tied up in a special conference. The kids never complained, but I could see the disappointment in their eyes.

I kept promising that I would have more time "next year." But the higher up the corporate ladder I climbed, the less time there seemed to be.

Suddenly they were no longer 9 and 11. They were 14 and 16. Teenagers. I didn't see my daughter the night she went out on her first date or my son's championship basketball game. Mom made excuses and I managed to telephone and talk to them before they left the house. I could hear the disappointment in their voices, but I explained as best I could.

Don't ask where the years have gone. Those little kids are 19 and 21 now and in college. I can't believe it. My job is less demanding, and I finally have time for them. But they have their own interests, and there is no time for me. To be perfectly honest, I'm a little hurt.[13]

He's hurt? How do you think his kids felt growing up?

The destiny of future generations is in your hands. The choices that you make with your family today will determine the quality of life in your family tree for generations to come. That's why one man can make a difference.

If you save your boys, it will be the greatest and most fulfilling task of your life.

ONE GOOD MAN

The decade of the sixties was a time when a lot of young men rebelled against their fathers. Anarchy, dope, easy sex, and rebellion were in vogue on the college campus. As David Crosby, of Crosby, Stills, Nash & Young, is said to have commented, "Anybody who says he clearly remembers the '60s obviously wasn't there."

Yet I know of three men who made it through that era virtually unscathed. What is interesting is that each of them had a father who trained him in the essentials of life. A dad who was a strong male role model.

Each of these men was raised in a Christian home. After going off to college, they maintained their faith in Jesus Christ. Instead of rebelling against their faith, they grew in it. It is more than coincidence that each of these three men had a father who was committed to Jesus Christ.

By the way, there's something I failed to mention. Each of these three men had the same father. I know—I'm one of the three. What Steve Farrar, Mike Farrar, and Jeff Farrar have in common is Jim Farrar. We are all products of his leadership.

None of us choose our families or our fathers. But thanks to God's grace in our lives, the three of us were given a dad who modeled masculinity and leadership. He wasn't perfect. He'd tell you that. He tended to be irritable and impatient when he was tired. (That's where we got it.)

Don't get me wrong. Our family was not a perfect family. We had our disappointments, setbacks, and failures. In our family, everyone is a sinner. But the Lord Jesus came to save sinners. Dad taught us that.

He was very consistent, and each of us grew up to emulate his example. He married a lovely woman named Beverly, so each of us married lovely women named Beverly. (Well, we each found a lovely woman, but they wouldn't go for the name change.)

He showed us what it meant to be a man. A genuine Christian man. A man who loves Jesus Christ, his wife, and his kids. He showed us how to do that. And humanly speaking, that's all any son could ask.

That's what the rest of this book is about. It's about *how* to be a male role model. Perhaps you haven't had a role model who gave you a clear idea of what you are to be as a husband or father. As a result, you don't have the confidence you'd like to have in your role as family leader.

Let me make you a promise: this book will help you fill in the blanks on what it means to lead a family. With the help of the Holy Spirit, you will be better equipped to save your boys.

One man can make all the difference. I know firsthand the difference one man can make.

Ten years ago, in a quiet hospital room on the central California coast, I was able to remind him of that just a few hours before he entered into the presence of the Lord Jesus Christ.

That was quite a day.

As far as I know, my dad never planned on writing a book to men about saving their boys. He was a real estate broker for more than fifty years. Writing books was not his thing. But you should know something: he's the real author of this book.

I just watched him and wrote it all down.

REAL MEN DON'T

The hand, that means to make another clean,
must not itself be dirty.

—Gregory

D o you remember the book *Real Men Don't Eat Quiche*?
It had some great one-liners on the definitive characteristics of a real man:

- Real Men don't floss.
- Real Men don't buy flight insurance.
- They don't play Frisbee.
- Real Men don't use ZIP codes.[1]

And in my opinion, real men don't call for a fair catch.

As I recall, there was also a light bulb joke going around
about real men. Do you know how many real men it takes to

change a light bulb? "None. Real Men aren't afraid of the dark."[2]

I'd like to add a couple more one-liners. But these aren't funny. They're critically important to the survival of the family. *Real men save their boys.* And I can think of one thing in particular that real men must *not* do if they want to have any hope at all of saving their sons: *real men don't commit adultery.*

An epidemic of staggering proportions is taking place in America. I'm not thinking of COVID-19. I'm thinking of adultery. It's an epidemic that for the most part used to afflict only those outside the body of Christ. No longer. This epidemic not only has found its way inside the church but has also wormed its way up to the highest echelons of church leadership.

There's something strange about this epidemic, other than its rolling virtually unchecked through the body of Christ. What is strange is that we don't *call* it "adultery."

Author and architect Richard Saul Wurman got to the heart of the matter:

> Doublespeak is one of the biggest problems in the English language, according to a National Council of Teachers state-of-the-language report. They cited the following examples: One stockbroker called the October 1987 stock market crash a "fourth-quarter equity retreat." The Pacific Gas and Electric Company referred to its bills as "energy documents." The shutdown at the General Motors plant in Framingham, Massachusetts, was labeled by the company as a "volume-related production-schedule adjustment." A recent publi-

cation claimed that jumping off a building could lead to "sudden deceleration trauma."[3]

Let's cut the double-talk. Let's call adultery what it is. In the war on the family, adultery is treason. But we don't call it treason. We have developed a more refined and sophisticated term. Adultery has become an "affair."

When a man leaves his wife and children for another woman and acts as impulsively as an aroused junior high kid on his first date, it's not an "affair." It's adultery—and that's the blunt and unvarnished truth.

An *affair*. That word has sort of a nice, light, airy ring to it. Like quiche. It certainly isn't a judgmental term like *adultery*. The word *affair* is fluffy and nonthreatening. Affair is to adultery what quiche is to pot roast.

When I was a kid, I used to go to a fair. We would have a great time eating cotton candy, riding the Ferris wheel, and playing games at the arcade. When you went to a fair, you left all the responsibilities of normal life behind, at least for a few hours. Life was a lot of fun at a fair.

Maybe that's why we call adultery an affair. It's leaving behind your responsibilities. But let me say something about real men that I failed to mention earlier. Real men don't have affairs, because real men are responsible. Real men keep their commitments. Even when their personal needs are not being met the way that they would hope. Even when they are disappointed in their wives for some reason. In fact, that is precisely the time when we need to be on our guard more than ever.

Let's track this word *affair* for a minute. Dennis Rainey has come up with the best definition of an affair that I know of. According to him, an affair is an escape from reality, or a search for meaning outside the marriage.[4]

Ponder that definition for a minute. Think of the people you know personally who have been involved in an affair. Does that describe their motivation? It probably does.

Over the past several years, we have seen numerous Christian leaders exposed for adultery. It seems like hardly a month goes by that I don't hear of some pastor or ministry leader who has succumbed to the lure of an affair. No wonder we have a credibility crisis in Christianity.

Warren Wiersbe told of the great artist Raphael, who was painting his famous Vatican frescoes, when a couple of bureaucratic churchmen stopped by to watch and criticize:

> "The face of the apostle Paul is too red," said one.
> Raphael replied, "He blushes to see into whose hands the church has fallen."[5]

We have seen too many leaders in recent years who have preached righteousness from the pulpit with tremendous fervor while privately practicing unrighteousness in some hotel room with even greater intensity.

Righteousness must be found not only in our pulpits but also in our homes. The home is the church in miniature, and every Christian father has been appointed pastor of his own home. Christian men, whether they are leading in the church or in their homes, must seek after righteousness.

We all shake our heads when preachers proclaim one thing in public but do another in private. But adulterous acts aren't restricted to only those in full-time ministry. Those men just get more publicity. In this war, Christian men of all vocations are going down. Men who started well, men who were at one time committed to Jesus Christ and their families, walked into an ambush and destroyed their credibility and integrity. Enticed to pursue an affair, they now live every moment with the consequences of their treasonous act.

How do Christian men get pulled into adultery? And how can we protect ourselves from having the same tragedy happen to us? Scripture gave the antidote when it said, "Be very careful, then, how you live—not as unwise but as *wise*" (Ephesians 5:15, NIV).

Do you remember the old hymn "Rise Up, O Men of God"? Someone ought to write a new one titled "Wise Up, O Men of God." Whether you are a CPA, pastor, attorney, or salesman, an affair starts the same way. If we are to avoid the quicksand, we must wise up to the schemes of the enemy.

It usually begins with discontent. Things have changed—it's not the way it used to be between the two of you. You may have no explanation for it. Things are just . . . different. You don't seem to have the same good times you had when you were dating. You rarely enjoy good conversation. You're just not close. You eat at the same table, share the same bathroom, and sleep in the same bed, but you might as well be hundreds of miles apart.

If there's one word that describes your marriage, it's *distance*. There remains little sense of sharing anything in your lives. You simply coexist. The thrill is gone. Your marriage isn't just predictable; it's boring. And you are disappointed.

If there is a lack of sexual fulfillment, the frustration is especially acute, and a man who is not fulfilled sexually is especially vulnerable to outside temptation. Yet the sexual relationship is simply a reflection of the overall state of the marriage.

Remember the definition? An affair is "an escape from reality, or a search for meaning outside the marriage." Now, let's construct a typical scenario for an affair to take place in the life of a man who is either bored or frustrated with his marriage.

Perhaps you had never noticed her. But as you walked by her desk today, she looked up and smiled. Or maybe she's the new receptionist for a client you've been calling on for several years. Or perhaps a new project involves two different departments working together, and suddenly you're spending large amounts of time with a woman you didn't even know two weeks ago. Or maybe she's in the church and has come to you for counsel.

Whatever the reason or the circumstances, you now find yourself relating to another woman. She's attractive and a lot of fun to be around. She always looks like a million bucks. If you were single, you would definitely ask her out.

This is how an affair gets started. You're frustrated and disappointed with your wife. Your needs aren't being met. And then *she* comes along.

Here's where it gets tricky. It is what you do in these innocent situations that will either make or break you. If you don't make the right choices here, within a matter of weeks or even days, you are going to get emotionally hooked. And once you've swallowed a hook, it's almost impossible to spit it out.

How do you avoid taking the hook? Most men don't realize how vulnerable they are in these situations. Every marriage has its "down" times, and if a man doesn't recognize his increased vulnerability during these phases, he is sure to get himself in the deep weeds.

Author Randy Alcorn suggests that you ask some important questions to determine if there is a hook already lodged in your emotional jaw:

> Do I look forward in a special way to my appointments with this person? . . . Do I seek to meet with her away from my office in a more casual environment? Do I prefer that my coworkers not know I'm meeting with her again?[6]

If the answer to any of these questions is yes, then a red light should be flashing on your dashboard. What do you do if you find yourself in this kind of situation?

In battle, it is called "retreat."

Paul's instruction in 1 Corinthians 6:18 is to flee immorality. That's the *modus operandi* of the Christian man. That means back off, Jack. That means you stop having lunch with her. If you work together, then so be it. But don't do anything other than work. Stop taking side trips to go by her desk. She is Off-limits, with a capital O.

Let me point out something I've discovered in talking with men who find themselves in this type of scenario. Up until now, absolutely nothing has happened. *What's the harm?* they ask themselves. *We're just talking.* That is precisely the harm. Ninety-nine men out of a hundred don't realize they are being set up by the enemy.

The problem with getting together and talking is this: The woman will be interested in what you have to say. As you discuss your ideas and plans, you will undoubtedly find her to be remarkably engaged and encouraging. You will begin to sense an attitude of understanding and appreciation that perhaps you haven't gotten at home recently—or perhaps for a long time.

Whether you mean to or not, you will begin to compare her to your wife, and your wife is going to lose. Why will your wife lose? Because if there are needs in your life that your wife isn't currently meeting, and if this woman has a great deal of respect for you and interest in you, your wife can't help but come in second.

If you and your wife are struggling, this woman probably will be more understanding than your wife. But why is she more understanding? I hate to be the one who breaks the news, but it's probably because she doesn't know you very well. All she sees are your strong points, especially because you are working overtime to impress her. If she knew you as well as your wife does, would she be so understanding? I doubt it.

If a man saw clearly at this stage, he would realize that he's living in an unreal world. That, remember, is the definition of an affair. It is an escape from reality or a search for fulfillment outside marriage. The attraction is simply this: you are tired of fighting the battle at home, and with this new companion, there is no battle. That is the temptation. But look out! You're about to step on a land mine.

Do you see how subtle the enemy is? If some attractive woman were to walk into your office at 3:30 p.m., remove her clothes, and say, "Let's get physical!" you would call for security. That approach is too blatant. It repels rather than attracts. So the enemy doesn't use it.

But he constantly uses the approach we are discussing. He uses it for the same reason that billionaire sports-team owners spend millions on free agents. It works with bankers, stockbrokers, real estate agents, research technicians, and pastors. Many men have fallen through this subtle and seemingly harmless process.

What does a guy do when he wakes up and realizes he's on the verge of becoming emotionally hooked with another woman? I've talked with a number of men who have suddenly realized the implications of their emotional relationship. It has gone no further than an emotional attraction. No physical moves have been made. But it's decision time.

The choice at this point is to go one of two ways. The first is to realize that you are almost in over your head. You are in a very dangerous situation. You did not realize you were standing so close to the edge of the cliff. Suddenly it is clear. The decision must be made to back off, to nip this thing in the bud before it goes any further. And the decision must be made and acted on immediately. That is the rational and wise response.

The second response is what's called rationalization. When a guy says, "Hey, it's no big deal. We're just having lunch. I can handle it," then he has already taken the bait . . . hook, line, and sinker.

Commentator Boake Carter is often credited with saying that "in time of war, the first casualty is truth." Don't flatter yourself. You *can't* handle it. You are lying to your soul, and you are setting yourself up for the worst mistake of your life.

Alcorn wrote that "a relationship can be sexual long before it becomes erotic. Just because I'm not touching a woman, or just because I'm not envisioning specific erotic encounters, does not mean I'm not becoming sexually involved with her. The erotic is usually not the beginning but the culmination of sexual attraction."[7]

Does this feel like I'm reading your email? Are you involved in this kind of situation right now? If that is true, you are not alone. My guess is that there are hundreds of thousands of Christian men who either are currently in this situation or soon will be.

How can I know this? Because it is the primary approach the enemy uses to lure a man away from his marriage. His ways are so subtle and innocuous that most guys never realize they are about to become dead meat. Proverbs 7:21–23 (NIV) puts it this way:

> With persuasive words she led him astray;
> she seduced him with her smooth talk.
> All at once he followed her
> like an ox going to the slaughter,
> like a deer stepping into a noose
> till an arrow pierces his liver,
> like a bird darting into a snare,
> little knowing it will cost him his life.

I remember a lunch I had with a guy years ago. He was married, was in his late thirties, and had a couple of kids. He was an executive with a large ministry organization. He had been in the business world for a while and had recently taken a huge cut in pay to work for this Christian venture. By all outward appearances, he was a committed Christian with a sharp family.

As we were talking, I mentioned a book on marriage that I had just finished reading. He lit up. "I've been studying that book with a friend for the past six months, and it has helped both of our marriages," he said enthusiastically.

For the next ten minutes, he told me what he had been

learning in the study with his friend. "Yes," he said in summary, "I would recommend that book to anyone. It has helped me grow closer to my wife, and my friend to grow closer to her husband."

Suddenly a blip appeared on my radar screen. Did he say it helped his friend grow closer to *her husband*? For some reason, I had been assuming (and I think it was a fair assumption) that the "friend" was a he.

I have a sophisticated approach to counseling. Basically, if I find a scab, I pick it until it bleeds. I had definitely found a scab, so I picked.

I began to ask him some general questions about his marriage. Then I asked him about his friend. He made it clear she was a strong Christian and that their relationship was strictly platonic. But the more I probed, the more he backtracked. After several minutes, I thought it was time to be direct.

Usually whenever I want to ask someone a really personal question, I say, "Can I have your permission to ask you a personal question?" For some reason, people almost always say yes. He said yes too. So I asked him, "Why are you studying that book on marriage with someone else's wife? Have you ever thought of studying it with *your* wife?"

I should have guessed what was coming. "My wife doesn't understand me," he said.

"But your friend does understand you, right?"

"Yes, we can really communicate."

"May I ask you another pointed question?"

"Sure."

"Are you involved with your friend physically?"

"Of course not," he shot back.

"Have you kissed her yet?"

No reply.

"Can I take a guess who your friend is?"

"Oh, you don't know her."

"When I came into the office, there was a pretty blond receptionist. Tall, late twenties, very outgoing. Is that your friend?"

He didn't say anything; he just gazed out the window like a man looking for a bus that was an hour late. I had already pressed my luck, so once more wasn't going to hurt. "I'm not a prophet, but let me make a prediction. Within six months, you'll be in bed together."

He nearly came out of his chair. "That will never happen!"

"Sure it will. I may be off on the time, but it'll happen."

This guy was mad now. "That-will-never-happen," he seethed through clenched teeth.

As kindly as I could, I told him the reason it would happen was that he was convinced it *couldn't* happen. And pride always comes before the fall (see Proverbs 16:18). Tragically, it did happen.

By the way, it could happen to me. It could happen to you. It has happened to my friends and to yours. Better men than us have gone down. None of us are exempt. We are in spiritual warfare, and given the wrong circumstances, any one of us could go down at any time.

We are in the greatest danger of all when we think we are safe. When a guy begins to think that this could never happen to him, he needs to think again. I once heard Joe Aldrich make a statement that sent a chill down my spine. He said, "Have you ever noticed how many men in the Bible failed in the second half of life? Our enemy is so cunning that he will wait forty or even fifty years to set a trap." That's precisely what happened to King David.

You can never deceive yourself into thinking you are somehow "above" sexual sin. The moment you begin to view yourself in that light, you can be sure that one day your carcass will be hanging in cold storage.

I came on pretty strong with this guy. He was so far gone on this woman that my only hope of pulling him back was to hit him hard. He knew the Scriptures, and he knew in his heart of hearts that he was wrong. But it was too late. He had taken the hook. He was already dead meat. Within weeks he walked out on his family.

Another discarded wife. Two more shattered children. Another family for the casualty list. Why? Because he bought the lie that the grass is greener on the other side of the fence. But it never is. As someone has said, "The grass is always greener on the other side—that's because we can't see over the fence." But God can see over the fence, and when it comes to an adulterous relationship, He sees a lot of chaos, tears, heartbreak, and bitterness that can poison your family's well for generations.

The problem is simply this: When you leave your wife to commit adultery with another woman, you take yourself with you. And you are your biggest problem. I am my biggest problem. You are walking into this new relationship with the same personality, strengths, and weaknesses you have in your current marriage. And if you can't work out things with your current wife, what makes you think it will be any different with another woman? You are a major part of the problem, and, unfortunately, you must take yourself along with you.

Now, you may be thinking, *Hey, wait a minute! This all sounds great, but you don't understand my situation. I'm absolutely miserable. I'd be better off in prison than in this marriage.*

Are you saying any of the following things to yourself? "I'm in prison because . . .

my wife has refused to have sex with me for the past two years."

my wife has put on seventy-five pounds since our last child was born and although she used to be very attractive to me, I'm not physically attracted to her now at all."

my wife is my greatest critic—she doesn't support me or encourage me in any way."

my wife's primary pleasure in life is to put me down, especially in front of other people."

I know those kinds of situations are very real and painful. Let me give an abbreviated response here that speaks to this kind of seemingly hopeless situation. First of all, God knows your situation and understands it. He fully comprehends the extent of your misery. He understands the depth of your frustration.

Second, there is a tremendous phrase found in 1 Samuel 2:30 that has universal application to those who will live by it. In that verse, God gives a remarkably encouraging principle: "Those who honor Me I will honor."

I do not want to minimize your prison of circumstances, but I do want to remind you that you are not the first of

God's people to find themselves in prison. It may be a literal prison, a prison of leukemia, a prison of a wheelchair, or a prison of marriage. But if you will remain faithful, God will honor you. I believe that your misery can be replaced by joy as you remain faithful and trust Him to honor your faithfulness.

I'm not suggesting there is an easy, overnight solution to your problem. But I am suggesting that divorce or adultery is not the solution it appears to be. Even those outside the evangelical camp will tell you that. As writer Pat Conroy observed upon his own marriage's dissolution, "Each divorce is the death of a small civilization."[8]

There is nothing wrong with desiring happiness, but horrendous problems develop when we become disobedient to obtain it. God rewards the obedient, and He is able to do far more than any of us could ever ask or think (see Ephesians 3:20). He knows your situation. He has not forgotten you. And if you will remain faithful, you will see Him work on your behalf in ways you cannot fathom.

If you are on the freeway looking for true happiness, do not take the exit marked Adultery. It may look like a shortcut, but it isn't. It's a dead end. Keep driving until you find the exit marked Obedience. That's the only road that will get you to genuine happiness, even if it gets you there by a roundabout route.

What you are looking for cannot be found outside God's will. It is clearly not His will that you violate your marriage covenant.

If you think you have misery now, wait until you commit adultery or get a divorce. You will regret it for the rest of your life. When a man leaves his wife for an alliance with another woman, he is not only breaking God's commandment but also making a decision that will fuel and magnify his personal disappointment.

The lure of adultery is that another woman will truly meet your needs. And what makes adultery a lie is that no other woman on the face of the earth, no matter how alluring, interesting, or beautiful, has the capacity to fully meet the needs of another human being. That's why adultery is the ultimate hoax. It promises what it cannot deliver.

Real men protect themselves against adultery. Real men think seriously about the consequences of such an act. As they do, they ponder the facts, not the fantasies. They consider the long-range implications of having a fling. They count the cost. And that's why they don't do it. By any calculation you like, it just isn't worth it.

A POINTED QUESTION FOR ANY MAN IN THE TRAP

Let me address the man who is currently involved in adultery. You know it's wrong, and you want to stop. So what do you do? There is only one solution and that is to take *extreme action*. Author and educator Donald Joy was right: "Once a relationship has moved to genital contact, it will not be terminated so long as access to privacy remains."[9] In other words, you are going to have to bring in a trusted third party to help you break the relationship. The privacy and all the deceit must come to an end. If you continue to keep this sexual liaison private, you will never stop on your own.

You must go to your pastor or to another mature, wise Christian you respect and trust who can give you clear biblical steps for ending this destructive relationship. You must approach this confidant with complete honesty and a willingness to do whatever it takes to make things right.

You can be sure of one thing: if you don't take this step on your own, eventually your sin will find you out. This deception cannot go on indefinitely without someone finding out. I urge you to take the initiative. If you do, God will honor you for taking the hard step. If you don't, He will hound you as incessantly as He hounded David. David lived in deceit for a year before Nathan publicly confronted him (see chapters 11 and 12 of 2 Samuel). That was necessary because he refused to listen to the private voice of God in his heart.

CULTURAL DESENSITIZATION

I'm convinced that one of the reasons so many Christian guys fall is that we have become desensitized to the sin of adultery in our culture. It doesn't scare us. It doesn't shock us. We've become used to it. Now it only means that some guy was "trying to find himself." We describe it as a "momentary lapse of judgment."

Yet the fact of the matter is that adultery is truly an unspeakable act of betrayal. Adultery means that a man has sexual intercourse with a woman other than his wife. It means that they meet in some carefully chosen romantic hotel and violate the clear commandment of God. As the lights are low and the commandment of God is even dimmer, he proceeds to kiss and caress a woman other than his wife. It's just a matter of minutes before they are naked together in bed. At this point, there is no turning back. They are naked and not ashamed—but they should be. Within a few steamy, passionate moments, he will insert his penis into her vagina.

Did that last statement shock you? That was my full intention. The act of adultery is shocking. But we have become so desensitized to it that we need to be shocked. Did you expect to read such a graphic description of the sexual act in a Christian book? You may be offended that I used the terms *penis* and *vagina,* and I debated being so graphic. I decided to include these words because they prove the point. Most of us are more offended by the terms *penis* and *vagina* in a Christian book than we are by the term *adultery.* Adultery has lost its meaning. Sexual intercourse with another woman is a monstrous betrayal. But we hear about it at the office, we see it on TV, and we absorb it at the movies. As a result, it has lost its bite. There's nothing to it anymore.

Adultery has even become acceptable for spiritual leaders. I'm convinced that one of the reasons we have an epidemic of adultery by those in the pulpit is that it no longer carries severe consequences. And why is that? Because we no longer consider it a severe act.

When a gifted spiritual leader commits sexual sin, our greatest concern is how quickly he can be "restored to ministry." Having committed adultery used to mean that a man gave up the privilege of ministry. Now, with time off for good behavior, it means that after a year or so, he may reenter the pulpit and continue to minister. Engaging in adultery has become acceptable behavior for leaders in the evangelical church.

It is no mistake that in the Old Testament, God chose to

put the mark of His covenant with Israel on the male penis. He didn't put it on the arm or the elbow or the thigh. God demanded that every Jewish man be circumcised on his sexual organ to remind him of the fact that he belonged to God.

Too many evangelical pulpits are filled by men who have slept with women other than their wives. How many are there? I don't know, but one would be too many. Is it any wonder we are not having a greater impact on our culture for Christ?

Yes, there is forgiveness and grace for the one who has committed adultery. God offers pure forgiveness and grace to cover all our sins. We cannot afford to ever lose that principle. The church lost it for nearly fifteen hundred years until Martin Luther rediscovered it and brought about that historical earthquake that registered 9.0 on the spiritual Richter scale: the Reformation.

Robert Farrar Capon gave a play-by-play description of what happened when grace was rediscovered:

> The Reformation was a time when people went blind-staggering drunk because they had discovered, in the dusty basement of late medievalism, a whole cellarful of fifteen-hundred-year-old, 200-proof grace—of bottle after bottle of pure distillate of Scripture that would convince anyone that God saves us single-handed. . . . Grace was to be drunk neat: no water, no ice, and certainly no ginger ale.[10]

If you are reading this and adultery is in your past or in your present, know there is forgiveness available as you simply call upon the Lord with a repentant heart. But forgiveness does not automatically restore the privilege of spiritual leadership. Let me offer a critical principle: *in the New Testament, forgiveness is free, but leadership is earned.* It is earned by the power of a man's life. Sin, although forgiven, always sets off practical consequences. A mature spiritual leader who sins and repents is forgiven, but he is not exempt from the series of aftershocks that will come his way from his disobedience.

I carefully chose the word *mature* in the previous sentence. A young man in his teens or early twenties is in the stages of developing character; that's why we normally don't put him in the upper levels of leadership.

Many years ago, I had dinner with a group of men who all led various ministries. The average age was somewhere around forty. As we ate, the conversation turned to our conversions and some of the foolish and wrong things we did as young believers in college. There was drunkenness, cheating in school, drugs, sexual immorality, bar brawls, and a few other activities.

Let me hasten to add that the Lord disciplined every one of us as a father would discipline a young, immature son. God was disciplining us because He wanted to give us spiritual responsibilities.

My point is this: all of us in our youth did some pretty stupid things. I wouldn't think of driving a car at a speed of 105 miles per hour on the Bayshore Freeway south of San Francisco—especially on a Friday evening at seven. But that's exactly what I did with two friends many years ago.

Evangelist Billy Sunday is said to have observed that "a sinner can repent, but stupid is forever." That's a funny line, but we mustn't remain stupid forever. We expect people to grow up emotionally. We expect men over thirty to act differently than they did when they were under twenty.

That's why there is a difference between the sin of an immature believer and the sin of a mature one who is in leadership. And when a mature spiritual leader in the second half of his life commits sexual immorality, there are severe consequences. Please understand that I am not excusing sin at any age. I am saying, however, that those mature men who are in spiritual leadership are held to a higher standard. That's the crux of James 3:1: "Let not many of you become teachers, my brethren, knowing that as such we will incur a stricter judgment."

Pastor Chuck Swindoll hit the nail on the head:

> Ministry is a character profession. To put it bluntly, you can sleep around and still be a good brain surgeon. You can cheat on your mate and have little trouble continuing to practice law. Apparently, it is no problem to stay in politics and plagiarize. You can be a successful salesperson and cheat on your income tax. But you cannot do those things as a Christian or as a minister and continue enjoying the Lord's blessing. You must do right in order to have true integrity. If you can't come to terms with evil or break habits that continue to bring reproach to the name of Christ, please, do the Lord (and us in ministry) a favor and resign.[11]

King David was a real man—a man after God's own heart. But after committing adultery, he was never quite the same again. He was forgiven and wrote about it in psalms that continue to touch our lives thousands of years later. But the aftershocks devastated his family. His adultery was a detestable act, and God "set events in motion that would trouble David till his death."[12]

Some point out that David was allowed to keep his office of king even after his sexual sin. That's true. But in Israel, the king was not in "the ministry." He was a politician. The spiritual offices were prophet and priest. David didn't lose his office, because he didn't have a spiritual office. But, apparently, he did lose his razor-sharp edge of credibility, and until his dying day, he never completely got it back. One look at his family will underscore that.

A spiritual leader is to be a man above reproach (see 1 Timothy 3:2). Charles Haddon Spurgeon was the most influential preacher in England in the 1800s, yet his wisdom is still relevant today:

> I hold very stern opinions with regard to Christian men who have fallen into gross sin; I rejoice that they may be truly converted, and may be with mingled hope and caution received into the church; but I question, gravely question whether a man who has grossly sinned should be very readily restored to the pulpit. As John Angell James remarks, "When a preacher of righteousness has stood in the way of sinners, he should never again open his lips in the great congregation until his repentance is as notorious as his sin. . . ." My belief is that we should be *very slow* to help back to the pulpit men, who having been once tried, have proved themselves to have too little grace to stand the crucial test of ministerial life.[13]

I realize that you may not be in full-time ministry. But if you are a Christian husband and father who is serious about leading his family, then you *are* in the ministry. The offices of husband and father are also character professions.

The moral compromises in our churches and homes have got to stop. We have given ourselves permission to seek the company of other women if our wives aren't meeting our needs. We have lowered the biblical standards of holiness because we have been inappropriately influenced by our culture. We are the salt, and we have lost our saltiness. If we ever hope to raise moral standards outside the church, then we had better begin by raising them within the church.

I remember many years ago watching sportscaster Phyllis George interview Dallas Cowboys superstar Roger Staubach. It was a typical, dull sort of interview until she noted, "Roger, you have an all-American image. You're kind of a straight guy. Do you enjoy it, or is it a burden?"

Referring to her previous interview with Joe Namath, infamous for his "swinging" bachelor lifestyle, Staubach coolly responded, "I enjoy sex as much as Joe Namath, only I do it with one girl. But it's still fun."[14]

Touchdown! Roger hit the end zone with that comeback. Real men don't commit adultery. A real man sticks with one woman. Period.

4

A ONE-WOMAN KIND OF MAN

I can resist everything except temptation.

—*Oscar Wilde*

Hernán Cortés had a plan.

He wanted to lead an expedition into Mexico to capture its vast treasures. When he told the Spanish governor his strategy, the governor got so excited that he gave him eleven ships and seven hundred men. Little did the governor know that Cortés had failed to tell him the entire plan.

After months of travel, the eleven ships landed in Veracruz in the spring of 1519. As soon as the men unloaded the ships, Cortés instituted the rest of his plan. He burned the ships.

That's what you call commitment. That's what you call no turning back. That's what you call burning your bridges. By burning the ships, Cortés eliminated the options. There would be no back door, escape hatch, or parachute. He didn't know what he would encounter on his expeditions to the interior. He didn't know the strength of the people he would be fighting. But he did know this: there was now no escape for his men. In one fell swoop, he had not only eliminated their options but also created an intensely powerful motivation to succeed. Like it or not, they were now committed.

Guys, if we are going to save the boys, then we must save our marriages. And there is only one way to save our marriages: burn our ships. That expresses commitment, which says that no matter what comes in the future, you're going to stick it out. Commitment means that you have obligated yourself to follow through on your word. It's your personal guarantee that you will do what you promised.

Years ago when I was pastoring, a man sat in my office. He was in his early sixties, had been married to the same woman for nearly forty years, and had five grown children and numerous grandchildren. He had been a committed Christian since coming to Christ in high school. For years, he had been a pillar in the evangelical community, serving as a leader in his church as well as on the boards of various Christian ministries. He had an excellent grasp of the Scriptures and had influenced hundreds of young people for Christ.

Why were we meeting? To discuss his teaching a Bible class for men? To look into the possibility of his mentoring some younger men in the church? No. We were meeting to discuss why he'd been involved in an immoral relationship for five years with a woman younger than his daughters.

He wasn't denying his sin. A sharp thinker, he even had tight rationalizations that included scriptural references. As I continued to probe and slice through his web of excuses, finally, after about thirty minutes, he heaved a great sigh, slammed his fist on my desk, and blurted out, "Don't I have a right to be happy?"

That statement captured the spirit of our age.

We live in an era where commitment is cheap. It's cheap in marriage, business, politics, and even athletics. Commitment is cheap in professional sports when a running back will sign a six-year multimillion-dollar contract and then stay out of training camp in his third year because the team won't renegotiate his contract. Why does he want to renegotiate? Because some other backs in the league recently signed new contracts worth more than his. He wants to renegotiate because his contract is no longer personally convenient, and he refuses to keep his commitment until he gets his way.

Newspaper columnist Burton Hillis once said, "There's a mighty big difference between good, sound reasons and reasons that sound good."[1] Generally speaking, our society believes that only one commitment sounds good: *the right to be happy.*

Where were you in the turbulent sixties? I imagine you weren't around. More than likely it would be quite a while before you would be conceived and show up some nine months later.

But somewhere along the path of life, you probably heard from older family members or friends about that revolutionary decade that earthquaked our nation.

In 1967, I was a senior in high school on the San Francisco Peninsula, and I can well remember when multiple thousands of kids from all over the country flocked to the Haight-Ashbury district of the city by the bay. A cultural upheaval took place almost overnight. It was also the beginning of the sexual revolution that continues to this day.

We went from short hair to long hair. We traded our

cornflakes for granola and our Bass Weejuns for Earth Shoes. It was important during this time to be natural and hip. Nobody wanted to be "plastic." One of the best things you could do to demonstrate your "hipness" was to get several posters and put them up in your dorm room. It was not an easy choice. One poster shop could contain hundreds of posters. And the decision was critical: your poster must make the "right" statement.

Perhaps the most popular poster of that era portrayed a beautiful green pasture with rolling hills. The overall picture was slightly out of focus to give it an ethereal, vaporous look. There on the hill was a beautiful blonde with long, flowing hair. She wore a long, flowing dress and some beads. In the distance was a guy who (come to think of it) also had long, flowing hair and wore some beads. The whole scene was so hip and sixties-ish. But here's the clincher. Printed on the lower left side of the poster were these words:

> You do your thing, and I'll do mine,
> and if by chance we find each other,
> it's beautiful.[2]

That was so *together*! We thought it was *profound*!

Let me offer my own version of the poem, which would have been much more accurate:

> You be selfish, and I'll be selfish,
> and if by chance we find each other,
> it's nuclear war.

That's closer to reality! When I do my thing, I'm selfish. When you do your thing, you're selfish. That's not ultimate hipness. Doing your own thing and doing what comes naturally will ultimately destroy your marriage and your life. Human beings doing what comes naturally have caused all the crimes and wars and cruelties since Adam and Eve fell in the Garden of Eden.

The man sitting in my office never would have grown long hair, eaten granola, or traded his Florsheim Imperials for Earth Shoes. He was an established Christian businessman. But he swallowed the sixties' philosophy through and through. He was doing his own thing with this young girl, and he thought it was beautiful. He thought he had a right to be happy, and his right ended up destroying his family.

What about his wife of nearly forty years? Didn't she have a right to be happy too? But he never thought about that. He was blinded by his own lust for personal gratification and thus discarded—like a worn-out pair of Nikes—the woman to whom he'd once made a commitment.

On his wedding day, he said several significant things to that woman he ultimately judged to be obsolete. He promised to be committed to her in sickness and in health, for richer or poorer, for better or worse, until death would part them. On his wedding day, he said and did everything right. Except for one thing. He didn't burn his ships. Apparently, they were still in the harbor, loaded up for a fast retreat.

Advertisers are big on slogans and are paid a lot of money to think up memorable catchphrases to fill up the unclaimed nooks and crannies of your mind. They hope that if you can remember the slogan, you will remember the product it represents. Here are a few that I can't forget:

Melts in Your Mouth, Not in Your Hands

Just Do It

Keeps Going and Going and Going

You know the products, don't you? M&M's, Nike, and Energizer batteries. But let me call your attention to another slogan that may not be as familiar: *Semper Fidelis.*

More than two hundred years ago when the United States Marine Corps was being formed, much time was given to considering an appropriate motto. They finally chose the Latin phrase *Semper Fidelis. Semper Fidelis* is engraved on the mind of every United States marine. What does it mean? *Always Faithful.*

Those are two powerful words. But of the two, the first is the most important, for it explains how a marine is to be faithful. A marine is not to be faithful only when it's personally convenient or when the circumstances will guarantee his personal happiness. Instead, he will be *always* faithful, regardless of personal convenience or happiness.

That's why burning your ships is not a onetime event. It's not something you do only as you stand in a rented tuxedo before a group of your friends and family. Burning your ships is something you do every day of your life.

Did you run track in high school? Perhaps you ran the 95-meter sprint, or the 195-meter? I didn't run track myself, but I had several friends who did. And as I recall, none of them ran the 95 or the 195. Several of them, however, competed in the 100-meter sprint and the 200. My point: in marriage, as well as in the Christian life, it's not how you start that counts; it's how you finish. You can run your guts out for 95 meters and even lead the field, but if you stop five meters short, those 95 meters were an exercise in futility. Too many men in our society are running the 95-meter sprint in their marriages. Commitment means you suck it up and finish.

If we are going to save our boys, then we must make a personal commitment to finish the race. It is much better for a boy to learn the meaning of *Semper Fidelis* from the example of his father than from a drill sergeant in boot camp. A boy who has a father who is committed to his mother will have a tremendous advantage when he becomes a husband. He will have an intuitive understanding that his commitment in marriage is not a right to be happy but rather the intent to demonstrate a willingness to be responsible. Even when it's inconvenient. Even when it crowds out his personal happiness.

Burning your ships sounds great. But how do you do it?

The way to burn your ships in the war on the family is to become a one-woman kind of man. First Timothy 3:2 and Titus 1:6 describe this character qualification necessary for spiritual leaders in the church (elders and pastors). The same qualification is required for deacons (see 1 Timothy 3:12).

An elder is a spiritually mature man who gives oversight to the church with other qualified men. Both passages insist that an elder must be "the husband of one wife." That has led to much debate over whether a divorced man could serve in this position. It is not my purpose here to discuss that issue. Instead, I want to explain that the phrase "the husband of one wife" could be literally translated "a one-woman kind of man." That is really the sense of the statement. One of the primary qualifications for a leader in the church is that he must be a one-woman kind of man. A one-woman kind of man has adopted the motto *Semper Fidelis*. A one-woman kind of man reminds himself every day that he has burned his ships.

Maybe you had a father who was not committed to your

mother. Maybe he made it a practice to be involved from time to time with other women. Or maybe your father was committed to your mom but just wasn't around enough to model it for you. You may be confused about what a one-woman kind of man is simply because you've never seen one in action. Regardless of your relationship with your dad, let's review the qualities of a one-woman kind of man.

A ONE-WOMAN KIND OF MAN IS COMMITTED WITH HIS EYES

Have you ever heard the classic song "I Only Have Eyes for You"? It was recorded by everyone from the Flamingos to Art Garfunkel.

> Are the stars out tonight?
> I don't know if it's cloudy or bright
> I only have eyes for you, dear.[3]

That should be the theme song of every Christian man in America. But *having eyes for only your wife* doesn't mean that you don't see or notice other women. That's impossible. And yet, because of our commitment to be one-woman kind of men with our eyes, we don't look at other women in a way that would diminish our commitment to our wives. One-woman kind of men have purposefully cultivated a special kind of blindness to other women.

In the Old Testament, Job put it this way: "I made a covenant with my eyes not to look lustfully at a girl" (31:1, NIV). He was making a commitment to a special kind of blindness. He was burning his ships. He was talking *Semper Fidelis.*

Let's carefully observe what Job was saying here. He wasn't making a commitment to never *notice* an attractive female. That not only would be ludicrous but would require actual blindness. Good-looking girls and women are everywhere. You can't help but see them.

There is a difference, however, between seeing a beautiful woman and lusting after her. Job's point was simply this: there is a difference between a look and a *lustful* look. Somewhere in between those two "looks" is a clear intersection with a stop sign.

C. S. Lewis once said, "He that but looketh on a plate of ham and eggs to lust after it, hath already committed breakfast with it in his heart."[4] Whether it's an attractive woman or a heaping plate of cholesterol, the principle is the same: there is a difference between looking and looking with lust.

A one-woman kind of man is a man who demonstrates his commitment by disciplining his eyes. We are all familiar with the guy who can't walk one block without giving some woman the once-over from head to toe. He will even stop dead in his tracks in the flow of pedestrian traffic to turn and watch her as she goes by. Most of us are a little better socially adjusted than that.

When I was a rookie pastor in my first church, I met with a group of guys every Tuesday night. After the meeting, I went with one of them to a local coffee shop. It was the coldest night of the year, and I was freezing, so I did something I never did in those days: ordered a cup of hot coffee. I rarely drank coffee. In a year's time I might have drunk three or four cups max. I just didn't like the stuff. But on that particular night, as we sat there and talked, I was so cold that I had at least five cups, plus cream and sugar. I'm embarrassed to admit that never once did it cross my mind that all that caffeine and sugar was going to make sleep impossible.

I got home about ten thirty, watched the late sports on the news, and went to bed. I couldn't go to sleep; I was wide awake. After about an hour, I went downstairs and turned on *The Tonight Show*. When that was over, I went back to bed, but no luck. I was so wired on caffeine that I couldn't blink my eyes, let alone close them. So I got up and read the new *Sports Illustrated* that had come in the mail that afternoon. Now it was around 2:00 a.m., and I went upstairs to give sleep another try. At three o'clock, I got up to see if there was an old movie on the tube. There wasn't.

I was getting a little ticked by this time. I had read everything in the house, and there was nothing on TV. Then I got an idea. Now, remember that this was 1978. There was no internet and there were no websites. There were no twenty-four-hour cable news stations, and ESPN had yet to be invented. If you wanted to get the latest news, you would read a newspaper or a news magazine like *Time, Newsweek,* or *U.S. News & World Report.* That was it! So back then, every grocery store and corner convenience market had a big rack of magazines. My subscription to *Time* had recently run out, and I decided to visit the local twenty-four-hour convenience store to see if they had the new one. So off I went at 3:30 a.m. to find a *Time* magazine.

As I was looking for *Time,* I picked up *Newsweek* and flipped through it, then *U.S. News & World Report,* and before I realized it, I had picked up *Playboy* and was rapidly turning its pages. Suddenly I came to my senses and thought, *What in the world am I doing? What if my wife were to see me doing this, or someone in my congregation? What kind of pastor would do something like this? I'm standing here like some kind of adolescent trying to get some jollies.*

I felt utterly ashamed as I put down that magazine. I looked around and saw no one else in the store but the clerk. I assure you that I had not planned to pick up that magazine when I went into that store. But I did. I'd been picked off in a weak moment.

The next morning, I told my wife, Mary, what I had done—that wasn't easy. But I had to come clean with her and ask her forgiveness.

As I was preaching the next Sunday, one of my points dealt with integrity. I commented on how easy it is to teach the truth without applying it to your own life. My greatest fear is to fall into the trap of teaching the very thing I am disobeying. So I did something extreme. I told the congregation the whole story of what had happened to me on Tuesday night. I couldn't stand up in front of them and be a hypocrite. I asked them to forgive me for being such a poor example. And that extreme decision helped me never want to have that kind of humiliating experience again.

It was embarrassing to face my congregation, but I decided it was better to be embarrassed than to stand up there and preach a lie. I wanted to be honest and let them know that none of us are exempt from temptation at a weak moment.

I learned a valuable lesson from that situation. A one-woman kind of man *must* have a predetermined plan fixed in his mind so he can withstand the sneak attacks of the enemy. From that point on, I developed a plan for how I would handle resisting pornographic material before ever entering any store or newsstand. To defeat the sexual temptation that comes to me through my eyes, I had to anticipate and determine ahead of time how I would react.

Many guys really have a tough time when they're traveling away from home. I'm writing this in a hotel room in Chicago, hundreds of miles from my wife and most of the people who know me. A hotel room on the road can be a very dangerous place for a one-woman kind of man who is not prepared for battle.

Since I'm committed to a special kind of blind love, I must particularly cultivate that blindness away from home. I know I must do this because I know myself. And the self I know has a hard enough time even when I'm *not* away from home.

Can you imagine going on a business trip without your iPhone? How would you survive? How would you even begin to function without it? Back in the days before smartphones, the primary way to access porn was in your hotel room. As soon as you walked into your room and dropped your luggage on the bed, you would see a card on top of the TV advertising five pay-per-view movies—and usually at least two of them would be pornographic. I remember seeing that card hundreds of times. The temptation was that I could watch the porn *and no one would ever know.* My wife would never know, and neither would my kids. But when I had recited my vows to Mary years ago, I had burned my ships. And every time I walked into a hotel room, I had to burn them again.

Sometimes it takes extreme measures to be a one-woman kind of man with your eyes. Back in the pre-iPhone days, I read about a man who took unusual steps to maintain this special kind of blind love. If he was going to be in a hotel longer than three days, he would call the hotel and ask the manager to remove the TV from his room. Usually, the manager would say that he couldn't do that. The man would then politely point out that the maintenance man could do it in a matter of minutes. If the manager wanted this man's business, the TV would have to go.

The problem for most men is not *working* on the road. It is the *leisure time* we have on the road. Author W. M. Taylor exuded wisdom when he said, "Temptation rarely comes in working hours. It is in their leisure time that men are made or marred."[5]

Removing a TV set is extreme. But I respect such a man, and, more important, so does his wife. He knows himself and recognizes his weakness. He knows that after a long day of exhausting meetings or sales calls, he is especially susceptible with his leisure time.

Jesus Himself advocated taking extreme measures in certain situations:

> You have heard that it was said, "You shall not commit adultery"; but I say to you that everyone who looks at a woman with lust for her has already committed adultery with her in his heart. If your right eye makes you stumble, tear it out and throw it from you; for it is better for you to lose one of the parts of your body, than for your whole body to be thrown into hell. If your right hand makes you stumble, cut it off and throw it from you; for it is better for you to lose one of the parts of your body, than for your whole body to go into hell. (Matthew 5:27–30)

Notice that Jesus didn't say if your eye offends you, put on sunglasses. He didn't suggest that if your right hand causes you to stumble, put it in an Ace bandage. He used hyperbole to make a clear, forceful statement.

The obvious lesson is that you must deal with the source of the temptation. You can pluck your eye out if you want, but it might be more effective to take some measured actions of accountability that will make you think twice about biting the hook of temptation. The principle our Lord was teaching was simply this: there are times in the Christian life when extreme action is not only appropriate but necessary.

The most intense battlefield for men today is the internet. Porn hangs in some cloud out there, available at a moment's notice. But oftentimes it doesn't even wait for you; it pursues you. It shows up when you are searching some news site or googling instructions on how to build your back patio. It's the ultimate predator.

Here's the problem. Since 2007, I have carried a live grenade with me all the time. A smartphone or tablet is a spiritual grenade, with the potential to do great damage. You absolutely have to get control of it along with all your other tech devices. That's why a tool like Covenant Eyes is so important. You can install this on your devices and then each month your wife, or your accountability partner, gets an email with your entire history for that month. That's a great way of keeping you from pulling the pin on the grenade and doing damage to your marriage, your relationship with your kids, and, most important, your relationship with the Lord.

Your wife and kids should be able to ask you at any time to hand over your phone and let them check your history. If you have set the accountability boundaries in place, it is a major motivation not to pull the pin and go to some destructive porn website.

When you get home from business trips, put your bags

down and give your phone to your wife and let her check your history of websites visited while you were away. That will force you to explain your actions. It will also keep you from sin.

Extreme, you say? A little over the top, maybe? You bet. And that's exactly what Jesus was telling us to do. I can promise you this: if we don't get extreme with the temptation of our eyes, then it will get extreme with us.

Pornography isn't just dangerous to our marriages. It's addictive, right up there with meth and cocaine, only much cheaper and far more available. So many young men are becoming addicted every day. That's why extreme measures must be taken to be on top of it with our sons. We've got to protect them and prepare them.

Perhaps you are caught in the hellish web of porn addiction. More than anything, you need to wrestle it to the ground. Let me give you some suggestions from a few wise counselors:

1. *Tell someone else about your problem.* Someone you respect. Someone you can trust. Admitting the problem out loud is the hardest step to take.
2. *Become accountable to that person.* He should be a mature brother in Christ who has waged the same battle himself. Better yet, get into a small band of brothers. Lions don't go after the strongest prey. They pick out the ones who are the weakest, the ones who are *separated from the herd.* Are you separated from a band of brothers who will have your back and hold you accountable?
3. *Figure out your weakness.* What is the chink in your armor, the trigger that flips your addictive switch?

Satan, that prowling lion, will use anything—even something as innocuous as leisure time. Or it might be stress, anxiety, exhaustion, frustration, failure, or deep disappointment. A lonely man living in an unfulfilling marriage is both isolated and weak.

4. *Find the best available tools to help you wage this battle.* Check out Canopy (Canopy.us). This parental-control app for the internet has been called "the most effective technology on the planet to block pornography."[6]

5. *Head off deep feelings of shame and self-loathing.* A Christian man who becomes involved in habitual pornography use will inevitably feel a deep sense of shame. Satan will use that shame to stomp the life out of you. He wants you to lose hope so he can pull you deeper into addiction. The last thing he wants is for you to take your sin to the Lord and cry out to Him for help.

Please take heart in these words:

There were those who dwelt in darkness and in the
    shadow of death,
Prisoners in misery and chains. . . .
Then they cried out to the LORD in their trouble;
He saved them out of their distresses.
He brought them out of darkness and the shadow of
    death
And broke their bands apart.
Let them give thanks to the LORD for His
    lovingkindness,
And for His wonders to the sons of men!

For He has shattered gates of bronze
And cut bars of iron asunder. (Psalm 107:10, 13–16)

The Lord is able to shatter gates of bronze and cut asunder bars of iron.

Whatever you do, don't lose hope. And don't live alone in your addiction. Thousands of Christian men are struggling just like you. Take your addiction to the Lord. Cry out to Him for help. And get into the foxhole with brothers like you who are fighting the same good fight. Do it for your wife. Do it for your son. Do it for your daughter. Do it for you.

A ONE-WOMAN KIND OF MAN IS COMMITTED WITH HIS MIND

A major battlefield in spiritual warfare is the mind. The mind is the line of scrimmage in the Christian life, and whoever controls the line of scrimmage controls the game. The mind is where the enemy seeks to control us. If he can influence our minds, he can influence our behavior.

It was Franklin Jones who wrote, "What makes resisting temptation difficult for many people is they don't want to discourage it completely."[7]

The apostle Paul had a different kind of outlook:

> Though we live in the world, we do not wage war as the world does. The weapons we fight with are not the weapons of the world. On the contrary, they have divine power to demolish strongholds. We demolish arguments and every pretension that sets itself up against the knowledge of God, and we take

captive every thought to make it obedient to Christ.
(2 Corinthians 10:3–5, NIV)

Let me make a critical point here: *temptation itself is not sin but a call to battle.* In this battle, as in any other, the objective is to take as many captives as possible. Let's specifically apply Paul's admonition to the man who wants to be committed to his wife in his thought life. Such a man protects himself from thinking or fantasizing about other women. This is a constant and perpetual battle. Christian men will deal with this nearly every day of their lives.

Let's put this battle into perspective. First—and this is very important—*you cannot prevent wrong thoughts from coming into your mind.* That's temptation. It is not wrong to be tempted. Jesus was tempted but was without sin. You have not sinned when you are tempted. You should not feel guilty when you are tempted. If you do, that is false guilt. Genuine guilt is the result of sin.

Let's go back to the grenade analogy regarding your smartphone. Perhaps you're checking your contact list, when you suddenly get an unsolicited text clearly linked to a porn site. Sin has not taken place at this point for having received the text. Only *temptation* has taken place. Satan has just lobbed a grenade of temptation into your mind. It is not sin to be tempted. But it is sin if you pick up the grenade and pull the pin.

The thought that flashes through your mind in that moment, tugging at you to violate your commitment to Christ and your wife by clicking on the text, isn't sin either. *But what you do with that thought in the next microsecond will determine whether it will turn into sin.*

So far, you've only seen the ham and eggs. You haven't had breakfast.

As your eyes come into contact with the text and the tempter suggests you follow it up, you must make a choice. Do you give in to the wrong thought and allow your eyes and mind to do what is wrong, or do you take that thought captive to the obedience of Christ? There is no sin in seeing the ham and eggs. But if you decide to linger over the food on the plate, you have just committed breakfast in your heart.

James 1:13–15 spells it out like this:

> Let no one say when he is tempted, "I am being tempted by God"; for God cannot be tempted by evil, and He Himself does not tempt anyone. But each one is tempted when he is carried away and enticed by his own lust. Then when lust has conceived, it gives birth to sin; and when sin is accomplished, it brings forth death.

These wrong thoughts are the grenades of the enemy. He hurls them into your mind at the most unexpected and surprising moments. You cannot stop them from coming. But you can develop a habit of capturing them and turning them into opportunities to obey Christ.

Don't get discouraged if you are having a tough time with your thought life. It normally takes time to begin making progress. Learning to deal with wrong thoughts is like learning to dribble with your left hand.

Some of my fondest memories from thirty-plus years ago came from shooting baskets in the backyard with my kids.

Our small makeshift court on the patio was anything but regulation but just right for short, intense scrimmages and five-foot bank shots. One day I decided to help my son John develop skills using his left hand. John is right-handed, so as we played he would naturally dribble with his right hand and rarely attempted it with his left. When I encouraged him to try it, he hated it.

Then I decided to change my approach. John and I like to play one-on-one, so I decided to make a rule change. For every dribble with his left hand before making a basket, I would multiply the two points for the basket by the number of times he dribbled with his left hand. If he dribbled with his left hand three times, then the basket was worth six points instead of two.

I purposely guarded him by standing to his right, forcing him to take the opening to his left. At first, he got discouraged as the ball bounced off his foot and veered into the bushes. I remember his intense frustration in trying to learn this new and foreign skill. On more than one occasion, he blurted out, "I'll never get it!" Nevertheless, I continued to position myself so he had to drive to his left.

As the weeks went by, he started getting four-point baskets, and then six-pointers. After several months, he actually dribbled nine times with his left hand and scored. I was down 18 to 0, and he had taken only one shot.

A few summers later, John went to a morning basketball camp put on by the local college coach and his staff. When I got home one day, John was ecstatic. He told me about a drill they all did that morning. The coach put out six pylons spaced out over a half-court area. Each boy had to dribble around the pylons to half court with his right hand, then switch to his left coming back. John won the competition.

He said, "Dad, just about everybody could do it with their right hand, but they all slowed down coming back with their left."

Why did John win that competition? I'll tell you why. John won the drill because he had developed a new habit.

The point is this: learning to deal with your thought life is the spiritual equivalent of learning to dribble with your left hand. You will not be successful at first. You will feel overwhelmed, discouraged, and frustrated. You will begin to think you will never make progress. But slowly and surely, you will develop a new habit. As the old saying goes,

Sow a thought, reap an act;
Sow an act, reap a habit;
Sow a habit, reap character;
Sow a character, reap destiny.[8]

If you have spent twenty-five years giving in to sexual lust, don't expect to turn things around in three weeks. But if you keep "going to your left" in your thought life, eventually you won't have to think about it as much. You'll never be perfect, but you can develop some very strong automatic responses to sexual temptation.

As you work to capture your thoughts, you'll develop spiritual muscle and character. And as far as I can tell, there's only one way to do that: *aggressively attack*. You have to get aggressive in your approach to temptation. Too many of us have lowered our standards and given ourselves unspoken permission to fail with sexual temptation.

We have to act against sin as aggressively as Hall of Fame linebacker Dick Butkus did against fullbacks. Have you ever seen the YouTube video about his career?[9] His aggressive hitting was unbelievable. Jim Brown, who arguably was the greatest running back in football history, said, "Football is hitting. Butkus is the ultimate hitter."[10] Another NFL Hall of Famer, Deacon Jones, stated that "every time he hit you, he tried to put you in the cemetery, not the hospital."[11]

Why was Butkus so aggressive? Because his objective was to attack the ballcarrier. He didn't want to just tackle the runner; he wanted to remove the guy's helmet with his head. That's how we have to respond when sin comes calling.

There are two things you must do. First, look away from the temptation. You made a covenant with your eyes, remember? *Semper Fidelis.*

Second, let me suggest something completely wild. Immediately begin to pray for that woman. Seize the wrong thought and begin to pray that if she doesn't know Christ, she will come to know His love and forgiveness. If she's married, pray for the relationship she has with her husband—that their marriage would be protected from the attacks of the evil one. If she's single, pray that God would keep her pure and clean for the man she might someday marry.

I think you get the point: you cannot pray and lust at the same time.

A one-woman kind of man is committed with his eyes and with his thought life. But there are three other characteristics that complete our description of a one-woman man. These next three descriptions will be brief—just three vignettes. (By the way, that's how I like my salads . . . just a little oil and vignette.)

A ONE-WOMAN KIND OF MAN
IS COMMITTED WITH HIS LIPS

A man committed to his wife is no flirt. He doesn't play junior high games with other women. He doesn't kid around about being interested in someone else. He doesn't make jokes about getting together with other women.

Such jesting can all come under the umbrella of having a few harmless laughs. But some things are off-limits as humor sources. Marriage is one of them. Marriage is sacred. Marriage is holy. It's nothing to kid around about.

A ONE-WOMAN KIND OF MAN
IS COMMITTED WITH HIS HANDS

When I was a kid, my mom used to tell me to keep my hands to myself. Usually, I had just criminally assaulted one of my brothers.

"Keep your hands to yourself" is a great piece of advice if you want to be a one-woman kind of man. A one-woman man is careful how he touches the opposite sex. Why is he careful? Because he's committed to one woman. *Semper Fidelis.*

As a rule of thumb, I usually don't hug other women. That presents a problem because a lot of Christians like to hug. Often when I refuse a hug, it pushes somebody's button and the other person gets upset and thinks I'm not loving or kind. But that's not it.

Mary and I have some close friends we love dearly. When we run into one another, it's not uncommon for me to hug my friend's wife as a greeting and for him to hug Mary. But generally speaking, I don't hug women. Why not? Because I want to be a one-woman kind of man, and the way I figure it, that means hugging one woman.

The real reason I'm bringing this up is that I've noticed a correlation between verbal flirting and flirting that includes touching, even "harmless" touching. I knew one church deacon who, with his wife, greeted everyone at the door on Sunday mornings. I watched his wife's embarrassed expression as he would hug and stroke (in a spiritual way) every attractive woman who arrived. He was always joking around about wanting to meet the woman at a hotel or get together for dinner. He was "just kidding," of course.

I guess that's why I wasn't surprised when he ran off with the youth director's wife. He never was a one-woman kind of man, and it showed.

You know as well as I do that a hug can come from the purest of motives. But it can also come from wrong motives. There's nothing wrong with a hug. But the next time you think about hugging a woman and you're not sure about your motives, don't do it. If you want to hug somebody, go find your wife.

A ONE-WOMAN KIND OF MAN IS COMMITTED WITH HIS FEET

First Corinthians 6:18 says it flat out: "Flee from sexual immorality" (NIV). That's how a one-woman man deals with movies, magazines, videos, and any kind of situation that is counterproductive to marriage commitment. He flees.

Someone has said that most men who flee temptation usually leave a forwarding address. That won't cut it if you're going to be a one-woman kind of man. A one-woman man doesn't hang around to check out a pornographic magazine for its artistic value. He doesn't hesitate to walk out of a movie that violates his value system. He takes the lead in turning off a program on Netflix. That's what it means to flee. A one-woman man uses his feet to demonstrate his commitment.

Well, that's it. That's what a one-woman man looks like. He burns his ships. He practices *Semper Fidelis*. He hits wrong thoughts like Butkus after a wide receiver. He has eyes for only her, his lips are sealed, his hands are tied, and his feet are quick. That's the kind of energy it takes to stay away from adultery. Such energy is supplied to only those men who watch their nutrition and diet carefully. And I'm not talking about meat and potatoes.

5

ANOREXIC MEN AND THEIR BULIMIC COUSINS

We owe the Scripture the same reverence
which we owe to God.

—*John Calvin*

A lot of pop music stars die young. It seems to go with the territory. Whether it's from a plane crash or a drug overdose, it seems to happen frequently.

You know about anorexia, right? Of course you do. Everyone knows about anorexia. It's a horrible eating disorder that primarily afflicts young women and can literally kill them.

In January 2020, generally speaking, nobody knew about COVID-19. By March 2020, everybody in the world knew about it and was looking for a mask and hand sanitizer.

Back in the beginning of the eighties, the average person in America had never heard of anorexia. But that literally changed in one day. Suddenly everyone—and I do mean everyone—knew about anorexia.

On February 4, 1983, the news came out that one of the bigger pop music stars in the world, Karen Carpenter, had died at the age of thirty-two. Even more baffling was what had killed her. It wasn't a plane crash or drug overdose. She had died from a heart attack brought on by *anorexia nervosa*.[1] And when people heard the cause of her death, they said, "What in the world is that?"

Karen Carpenter had been anorexic for years, and most of us had no idea what the illness was.

Anorexia nervosa is extreme body emaciation caused by an emotional or psychological aversion to food and eating.[2] The condition occurs predominantly in young women whose body weight has dropped to half of normal. In contrast to victims of famine, sufferers of anorexia nervosa are often able to maintain their strength and daily activities at approximately normal levels. They appear to be unconcerned with their undernourished state and do not feel hungry. In layman's terms, a person with anorexia nervosa avoids food.

I'm convinced there is such a thing as spiritual anorexia—and the enemy has been incredibly successful at spreading it. In the spiritual realm, it is not partial to women. Thousands of Christian men have spiritual anorexia, and that is why they are ineffective in leading their families. What is spiritual anorexia? *Spiritual anorexia is an aversion to reading the Scriptures and digesting them.*

We all have seen tragic pictures of starving children in foreign countries. Many of them are so weak they cannot stand up. Spiritually anorexic men have something in common with those children: they all lack nutritious food.

The words of Jesus recorded in Matthew 4:4 prove the point: "Man does not live on bread alone, but on *every word* that comes from the mouth of God" (NIV). Scripture contains all the nutrients that will keep you spiritually alive and powerful, equipped for the task of leadership.

Carefully observe the words of Deuteronomy 32:46–47: "Take to heart all the words I have solemnly declared to you this day, so that you may command your children to obey carefully all the words of this law. They are not just idle words for you—they *are your life*" (NIV).

The Lord is saying that His Word is your very life.

I'm going to be up front with you: this is a dangerous chapter. It's dangerous for *the enemy* if you read it and take it to heart, and it's dangerous for *you* if you don't.

The man who takes up "the sword of the Spirit, which is the word of God" (Ephesians 6:17) is well armed in the battle against Satan, and our enemy knows it. That's why he will do whatever he can to keep you from reading this chapter, much less taking it seriously.

Earlier I mentioned that the enemy has two primary strategies in the war on the family. The first is to effectively alienate and sever the relationship between husband and wife. The second is to effectively alienate and sever the relationship between father and children. But there is a third strategy he uses with deadly effectiveness.

Strategy #3: *To effectively sever and alienate a man from the spiritual disciplines that will keep him fit and effective for spiritual battle.*

Satan doesn't care if you go to church and fill your life with good activities. He knows that if he can keep you busy

24/7, if he can distract you from spending time with the Lord and feeding off Scripture, *you will starve to death spiritually*. That's how he will keep you from becoming the spiritual oak your family needs.

No wonder the enemy wants to keep us from the Scriptures.

C. S. Lewis wrote a wonderful little book titled *The Screwtape Letters*. The book records the letters of an old and wise demon, Screwtape, to his young nephew, Wormwood—a rookie at spiritual warfare. Wormwood has been assigned to influence a certain man away from Christianity. Lewis cleverly and humorously described the different methods the enemy will employ to keep us from any kind of spiritual growth. It's a wonderful book that contains much insight and wisdom.

But as the great pastor and author Martyn Lloyd-Jones pointed out, the book has one major defect. Lewis does not deal with the question of reading the Word of God—the crafty old uncle gives no instruction to his young nephew about keeping his intended victim away from the Bible.[3]

Yet this is precisely what the enemy attempts to do and may be his primary goal. He will go to any extreme to keep us from taking in Scripture. This is one of his most consistent tactics, and he is relentless in it. He does not want us reading God's Word; he wants us spiritually anorexic.

George Gallup, the famous pollster and committed Christian, was asked in an interview for *Leadership* journal whether any of his poll results had surprised him. "Oh yes," he answered. "I'm amazed . . . at the low level of Bible knowledge. It's shocking to see that only 42 percent know that Jesus was the one who delivered the Sermon on the Mount. . . . Are they reading the Bible? From our studies, the Bible is clearly not being read. It's revered, but not read."[4]

Gallup described spiritual anorexia. The vast majority of Christian men I know who are spiritual anorexics believe that the Bible is inspired by God. Most of them own several translations of the Bible, including at least one study Bible. They also have Bible apps on their phones. They hold the Bible in high esteem, yet they rarely read it. Except on the big screen or their smartphones at church.

For a number of years, I was a spiritual anorexic. I wasn't growing in my Christian life, and no wonder. My intake of the Word was hit and miss. I always meant to read the Scriptures, but somehow other things crowded out my time. I would plan on reading the Bible just before I went to sleep, but by the time I hit the sack, I was just too tired. *I'll get up early and do it in the morning,* I would say to myself. But when morning came, my Scripture reading got crowded out again. Day after day, week after week, month after month, I had the best of intentions. But somehow I never got into a consistent pattern. It took several years before I realized I was starving for spiritual nutrition. I had to change my priorities.

As a result, I made a personal commitment to begin each day by reading Scripture. I've been doing this now for years, yet every single morning, I am tempted to skip my reading. Amazing! Allow me to describe the situation.

There is a famous opening statement that crawls across the screen at the beginning of most every Star Wars movie: *"A long time ago in a galaxy far, far away . . ."* And then comes the next paragraph with the background and context needed to understand this new chapter of the Star Wars universe. That background information is very important, since George Lucas released the movies out of sequence.

In our discussion of the priority of reading Scripture—and the temptation to not read it—I'd like to tweak that famous crawl line: *A long time ago in a generation far, far away, there was something called a newspaper.* Newspapers are still around, of course, but are becoming increasingly rare—or at least the printed versions are. Most newspapers now have online versions for those who don't want to search for the paper copy lodged somewhere behind a rosebush near the front porch. So even though newspapers have now gone digital, they can still be a viable threat to someone like me who wants to start the day by reading God's Word.

It used to be that every morning, I was tempted to immediately open the front door, locate my newspaper, grab my coffee, and dive headfirst into the news of the day. Now the scenario is a little different. The news is delivered online to my phone, tablet, or desktop computer, which makes it easier to give in to temptation and skip the Bible reading.

Every morning at home, as I get out of bed and head for the coffee maker (despite the earlier story about my never drinking coffee, when I hit midlife, I experienced a coffee conversion), I have to make a significant decision. What I *want* to do is grab my phone and start checking the news and sports online. What I *need* to do is get my Bible off my desk and open it up. Every single morning, it's the same dilemma! You'd think it would get easier the longer I make that choice. But it doesn't, at least not for me.

I consider my time in the Word to be a morning briefing. Before I go out to face the day, I need to be briefed by the Lord. But what if you're not a morning person? I know several mature Christian men who are more effective at night than early in the morning. If that's you, just follow their pattern and do your briefing in the evening. It's not the time of day that matters.

The briefing serves different functions.

First, *it reminds me that there is a God who is ruling the affairs of my life.* Society lives as though there is no God, and I need to be reminded before I face the day that there is a God who is in control of my life and circumstances.

Second, *I need to be reminded of what is true.* God's Word gives me a dose of reality. There is right and wrong, there are consequences for making wrong choices, the Ten Commandments are still the standard for life, I am not to repay evil for evil, and much more. My morning briefing gives a perspective that I don't get in the world. I need God's commentary on life every day.

A Christian man in this culture is swimming upstream. Without the constant nutrition of the Word, he will soon tire and be dragged off by the force of the current. A solid education of biblical truth is not optional for the family leader. Samuel Johnson put it this way: "The supreme end of education is expert discernment in all things—the power to tell the good from the bad, the genuine from the counterfeit, and to prefer the good and the genuine to the bad and the counterfeit."[5] The Bible gives me that discernment every morning when I open its pages.

Third, *the morning briefing reinforces my convictions.* It's not easy to hold on to convictions when you're in the minority. You and I live in a society that is constantly trying to chip away at our biblical convictions. My time in the Scriptures each morning underscores why I hold those convictions. We are in a war for our families, and we cannot afford to compromise the divine absolutes given us. When a soldier begins to question his convictions about the morality of his cause, his effectiveness vanishes. That's precisely what happened to some of our soldiers a generation ago in Vietnam.

As I read the Scriptures, I am forced to evaluate my convictions. Perhaps some of them don't agree with God's Word and need to be changed. Or maybe I've started to compromise convictions I've always held. As I am exposed to Scripture, I find encouragement to stand firm in the truth and not negotiate what the Bible clearly teaches. Each day I have to make choices based on my convictions. That is why it is vital not to miss my morning briefing. I need God's input to make consistently right choices.

I cannot afford to be spiritually anorexic when I've been given the responsibility to lead my family. A malnourished man is worthless in hand-to-hand combat. Because he has no strength, he is easy prey for the enemy.

BULIMIC MEN

Anorexia is dangerous, but something else afflicts Christian men even more: spiritual bulimia.

To understand spiritual bulimia, we must take a look at the physical variety. Dr. Raymond Vath described it this way: "Bulimia is an illness with recurrent, compulsive episodes of binge eating followed by self-induced vomiting and/or purging with laxatives."[6]

Nice, eh?

This disorder, too, normally afflicts young women. Someone with bulimia will binge and take in a tremendous amount of food, only to quickly vomit, thus denying her body the nutrients it needs.

Spiritually speaking, bulimia is the consistent reading or hearing of the Word *without personal application*. The danger comes when I listen to a sermon or go to a Christian seminar or listen to a podcast without applying the truth I hear to my life. That is spiritual bulimia, and it's especially common among Christian men.

Spiritual bulimia is an aversion to applying the Scriptures to my life. Scriptural facts may be in my mind, but I am not integrating them into my life. I am chewing the food and swallowing it, but only for a while. Then I get rid of the food, preventing digestion. Without digestion, I cannot benefit from the nutrients in the food. Without meditation leading to application, there is no spiritual digestion, and I continue to lose strength.

Let me explain it from a different angle. The opposite of up is down. The opposite of happy is sad. The opposite of on is off. Now let me ask you something. What is the opposite of ignorance? "Knowledge," you say.

When people come to know Jesus Christ as Lord and Savior, they are spiritual infants. They are spiritually ignorant. That's why we put them in small-group Bible studies and suggest that they subscribe to some solid Bible-teaching podcasts. Those are all very good ideas. We do this so they can move from spiritual ignorance to spiritual knowledge.

But here is where we sometimes make a critical mistake . . . and open the door to spiritual bulimia. As the late, great professor Howard Hendricks pointed out, "In the spiritual realm, the opposite of ignorance is not knowledge but obedience."[7] God does not want to take a new Christian and move him from ignorance to knowledge. He wants to move him from ignorance to knowledge to *obedience.*

James 1:22 says, "Prove yourselves doers of the word, and not merely hearers who delude themselves." James was describing spiritual bulimia. The man who hears the Word of God has received knowledge. But knowledge is not the goal—the goal is to *do* the Word. The man must obey. Obedience means that I apply His Word to my life and circumstances. If I don't do that, then I am binging and purging.

Do you remember the two men I described earlier in this book? The first left a well-paying professional position to take a much smaller salary working for a Christian organization. He was the one studying the Christian book on marriage with his secretary. Chapter after chapter in that book identifies scriptural principles designed to help a man grow in his love for his wife. This guy read those chapters and got so excited that he would tell other people to buy the book. Then he would go where no one was watching and vomit up the scriptural truths that so excited him. He was a spiritual bulimic.

The second man I described was in his early sixties, a respected Christian leader in the community who left his wife of forty years for a woman younger than his daughters. That man was also a spiritual bulimic. He would sit in church every Sunday and listen carefully to make sure the sermon was doctrinally pure. Then he would go home, vomit the Word of God, and call his girlfriend. He knew the Word; he just didn't do it. That is spiritual bulimia.

Both men sought scriptural knowledge. Both appeared to have an appetite for spiritual truth. Both had "quiet times." And both left their families. Why? Because both thought the goal was to go from spiritual ignorance to spiritual knowledge. It isn't. The goal is to go from ignorance to knowledge to obedience. While they were both hearers of the Word, neither was a doer.

You don't have to commit adultery to be spiritually bulimic. A person has spiritual bulimia when he consistently refuses to apply a known scriptural principle to his life.

The biblical priest Ezra was neither anorexic nor bulimic. Scripture simply states that "Ezra had set his heart to study the law of the LORD and to practice it" (Ezra 7:10). That's what it means to be a spiritual self-starter: neither anorexic nor bulimic.

THE ANTIOXIDANT ALTERNATIVE
TO ANOREXIA AND BULIMIA

Psalm 1 deals with the issue of spiritual anorexia. This first psalm contains two key verses pertinent to our discussion. Let's note verse 2: "His delight is in the law of the LORD, and in His law he meditates day and night."

Psalm 1 contrasts the righteous man with the wicked man. One key characteristic of the righteous man is that he delights in the law of the Lord. The phrase "law of the LORD" is a synonym for the entire written revelation of God. The word *law* basically means "direction" or "instruction."[8]

The righteous man is not anorexic. He delights in getting clear direction from the Word of God, and this divine direction gives him satisfaction.

The key word in this verse is *meditates*. Warren Wiersbe said that "meditation is to the soul what digestion is to the body."[9] That is, meditation is spiritual digestion. If a man is either anorexic or bulimic, he will not meditate. And that means he receives none of Scripture's nourishment.

Meditation requires reading, but it is possible to read without meditating. The emphasis here is to read with understanding, to think about the significance of what God says in His Word. Such a man understands that Scripture is his source of spiritual instruction and nutrition, chock-full of spiritual vitamins and minerals. He knows it's his *only* source of spiritual nutrition.

The Bible is the meat and potatoes of our spiritual lives.

The Christian view of meditation is exactly the reverse of its Eastern rival. In the Eastern version, you empty your mind by chanting some meaningless syllable; in the Christian practice, you fill it with the truth of God's Word to contemplate the biblical ramifications for your life.

More than one hundred years ago, George Müller described the benefits of Christian meditation. Read this lengthy quote slowly and carefully to get the full significance of this great man's wisdom:

> I saw more clearly than ever, that the first great and primary business to which I ought to attend every day was, to have my soul happy in the Lord. The first thing to be concerned about was not, how much I might serve the Lord, how I might glorify the Lord; but how I might get my soul into a happy state, and *how my inner man might be nourished*. . . .
>
> *Now* I saw, that the most important thing I had to do was to give myself to the reading of the Word of God and to meditation on it, that thus my heart might be comforted, encouraged, warned, reproved, instructed; and that thus, whilst meditating, my heart might be brought into experimental, communion with the Lord. I began therefore, to meditate on the New Testament, from the beginning, early in the morning . . .
>
> . . . for the sake of obtaining food for my own soul.
>
> And yet now, since God has taught me this point, it is as plain to me as anything, that the first thing

the child of God has to do morning by morning is to *obtain food for his inner man.*

As the outward man is not fit for work for any length of time, except we take food, and as this is one of the first things we do in the morning, so it should be with the inner man. . . . Now what is the food for the inner man: not *prayer,* but the *Word of God:* and here again not the simple reading of the Word of God, so that it only passes through our minds, just as water runs through a pipe, but considering what we read, pondering over it, and applying it to our hearts.[10]

The antidote for spiritual anorexia and bulimia is scriptural meditation. Meditation enables us to digest the truth of God's Word. A superficial, quick reading of Scripture doesn't cut it. To use Müller's phrase, that's no different than water running through a pipe.

To sum this up, we're talking about making a spiritual plan to read Scripture and pray. There are four components to this plan:

1. *Plan a time.* You set the time that's best for you— morning or evening—and the Lord will be there.
2. *Plan a place.* What's a quiet place where you can think without interruption?
3. *Make a list.* This is your prayer list. Add anything that concerns you about any aspect of your life— your wife, your kids, government officials, your pastor—and anything else that is on your heart. Keep your prayer list short. Then pray for those concerns again when they come back to your mind.

Keep them specific instead of general. The Lord loves to answer specific prayers.

4. *Begin with Scripture.* For decades, Billy Graham started his day by reading five psalms and one chapter of Proverbs. That put him through Psalms and Proverbs every month. If you're looking for a good way to implement your plan, that might be a good way to start.

Are you feeling overwhelmed and discouraged in your walk with Christ? Are you defeated and spiritually ineffective? Have you lost your excitement and enthusiasm in following hard after Christ? Have you so given in to habitual sin that it now threatens to sink you? Have you been duped by the enemy into ignoring the Scriptures? Has your schedule become so crowded that you haven't picked up your Bible in weeks? As you step on the spiritual scales, do you find yourself weighing in at less than half of your normal weight? If so, you are starving for biblical food. The result is malnourishment and defeat.

You cannot live without the Bible. It is your life.

Don't lose heart! There is a way to turn it around, but you will not do so until you grasp several facts. To become a spiritual self-starter, you must develop a personal plan for spiritual growth.

Where do you begin? Let me offer several suggestions that others have found helpful. Ponder these carefully and then pick one or more that could work well for you. Each of them has the same objective: to give you time to interact with the Word and therefore enjoy a nourishing intake of divine wisdom.

1. Read Through the Bible in One Year

Have you ever tried this? Perhaps you started well in Genesis, made it through Exodus, and died a slow death in Leviticus. Several guides are available to keep this from happening. I have read the Bible through in a year multiple times. If this is of interest to you, I recommend you get *The One Year Bible* (published by Tyndale House), which will guide you through the entire Bible in one year. The text is divided into daily readings. Every day you read a section each from the Old Testament, the New Testament, Psalms, and Proverbs. The beauty of this is that you can start on any date and jump right into a systematized approach to the Scriptures. I highly recommend it.

If reading through the Bible seems overwhelming, then don't worry about it. The Bible is already broken down into sixty-six books, some large and some small, so there are plenty of other options to choose from. For instance, read through the gospel of John. This is a way to really get to know the Lord Jesus close-up. Read a chapter slowly and then stop and think about it.

Another book you could consider reading is Philippians. It's only four chapters, but it packs a mighty punch and is extremely relevant to every man I know.

You can always ask your pastor for a suggestion of what to read to help you get started. But this is something you don't want to put off. If you do, you're playing right into the enemy's hands.

2. Get a Good Study Bible

There are many excellent study Bibles available. The ESV Study Bible is outstanding. You can also access the ESV Bible through an app for your phone, tablet, or computer, and this app includes the MacArthur Study Bible and numerous other excellent biblical commentaries.

3. Listen to the Bible

In these revolutionary digital times, it's really easy to listen to God's Word wherever you are—working out or doing yard work or jogging on a trail. I already mentioned the ESV Bible app, which allows you to do that, and YouVersion's Bible App gives you the option of listening to a variety of Bible translations.

If you have a long commute, consider accessing these through a Bluetooth connection in your car. Or if you're an old guy who thinks that Bluetooth is a dental disease, you can still get the Bible on CDs.

4. Start a Scripture Memory Program

One of the best ways to lodge the Scriptures in your mind is with the *Topical Memory System,* published by the Navigators. This is a convenient set of small cards with printed verses that you can carry in your wallet or keep on the dash of your car. It comes with a guidebook to get you started. Thousands of men all over the world have used this valuable tool.[11]

5. Form a Small Accountability Group

I've seen guys all over the country form a small accountability group. This is simply a group of guys who get together either every week or every two weeks for breakfast or lunch. It can be two guys or five guys, but not much more than that. The purpose is simply to get together and check in with one another.

Tremendous personal benefits come from the practice of scriptural meditation. When you took your current job, undoubtedly one of the things you looked at closely was the benefits package. The benefits package of Psalm 1 is incomparable.

The package, offered to everyone who meditates on God's Word, is described in verse 3: "He will be like a tree firmly planted by streams of water, which yields its fruit in its season and its leaf does not wither; and in whatever he does, he prospers."

The man who meditates on the Word of God is like a mature, magnificent tree. Such a tree not only is impressive in strength, but it's also a thing of beauty. The next time you get an opportunity, go outside and walk around the block. Look for the largest tree on your street, and then take a few minutes to scope it out in detail.

A fully developed oak tree is a magnificent specimen of God's creation. We are impressed with its commanding and imposing presence. That describes precisely the man who has his roots sunk deep into the truth of God's Word.

Did you know that the most critical part of a tree is its root system? Though many folks believe "a tree's spreading superstructure is matched by its underpinnings, in fact the two are not mirror images; the roots may run out as far as three times the crown. . . . A typical forty-foot tall tree every day takes in fifty gallons of dissolved nutrients from the soil."[12]

We can look at only the part of the tree that is above the ground. But the amazing thing about such a tree is what is underground. That's precisely the point the writer makes in

Psalm 1. A man who wants to be spiritually mature must put his roots deep in the Word of God. Growth comes no other way. No wonder the enemy tries to keep us away from the Bible.

I grew up in a home with an oak tree right in the middle of the house. It wasn't a red oak, a black oak, or even a white oak. It's the kind of oak described in Isaiah 61:3, and it's called an oak of righteousness. I'm referring to my dad, who is now with the Lord.

Please note that I didn't call him an oak of perfection. But in my opinion, he was an oak of righteousness. He was a businessman who weathered some really scary storms. People in real estate know it tends to be feast or famine.

When my dad was in his early forties, he lost everything. Wiped out financially, he had to start all over—with three boys soon entering college. It's one thing to be at square one when you're twenty-one; it's quite another when you're forty-three.

I watched him as he saw everything he had collapse. He went from having assets to having nothing but liabilities. He went from a new spacious home to a small apartment. He literally went from a Cadillac to a Volkswagen. He went from being near the top of the ladder to the bottom.

That's hard on a man. Every day when my dad got up, misery and disappointment were waiting for him. Most of us deal with a fear of failure, but my dad actually experienced business failure. I'm sure he was embarrassed and humiliated. That's how I would have felt. Maybe you know what that feels like. Perhaps even now you are going through similar circumstances.

But you should know something about this catastrophe: my dad never stopped being an oak. Because of their mighty root system, oaks can withstand storms that uproot other trees. That might perfectly describe my dad.

The great fighter Joe Louis once said, "I don't like money, actually, but it quiets my nerves." But what do you do when the money isn't there? How do you quiet your nerves when one look at your checkbook opens the acid valve to your stomach?

For as long as I can remember, my dad got up at 5:45 a.m. to meet with the Lord. That was a standing daily appointment he kept for decades. The very first thing he did each morning was pick up his Bible, worn and used, its margins full of notes and its pages frayed.

I can remember several times as a little boy waking up early and going into the living room to see my dad kneeling in front of the couch with his Bible open in front of him. While it was still dark, he was taking in his fifty gallons of nutrients from the soil of God's Word. He stood tall and survived because he had a mighty root system.

I've written about my dad for four reasons. First, because it was a privilege to grow up in a home with an oak of righteousness. Some people in the Midwest have never seen the ocean. Others have never seen a giant redwood. Still others, no doubt, have never seen an oak of righteousness. I was raised by one.

Second, I'm writing about my dad because I saw that the secret to surviving the storms of life is to have a large taproot that goes deep into the Scriptures. My dad's business may have been failing, but his leadership at home was even stronger during this tough time. As a result, our family was never more secure or stable than it was during this difficult season. The test of leadership is crisis. My dad passed the test because he checked the field manual every day.

Third, I'm sharing my dad's story because right now you might be in the biggest storm of your life. I'm urging you to get your roots deep into the Bible. That's what will keep you strong and steady in the storm. The Lord is not trying to ruin you; He is rebuilding you. But you must digest His Word to stay strong. Don't lose heart. You *will* make it because Christ is with you. He still knows how to calm the storm. At the right time, He'll calm your storm too.

Fourth, I have written about Dad because none of us know what the future holds. None of us are financially secure—although we may think we are. None of us are emotionally secure. None of us have a guarantee of health. Consciously or subconsciously, we think we are exempt from certain hardships in life, maybe because to this point in life we've escaped them. But there are no guarantees.

In the years following that big storm, God gave it all back to my dad, restoring the years the locusts had eaten (see Joel 2:25). In his later years, he was financially restored because of the Lord's faithfulness. He certainly wasn't wealthy, but he was comfortable. But even if he had lost it all again, it wouldn't have shaken him. His roots were just too deep.

And when the roots are that deep, it has a way of quieting the nerves.

6

HUSBAND AND WIFE TEAMWORK IN THE MARRIAGE COCKPIT

> Two are better than one,
>   because they have a good return for their work:
> If one falls down,
>   his friend can help him up.
> But pity the man who falls
>   and has no one to help him up!
>
> —*Ecclesiastes 4:9-10, NIV*

I do a fair amount of flying. That's why I almost had a coronary when I read a report on the crash of Continental Airlines Flight 1713.

It had been snowing hard in Denver on the day of the crash. That's nothing unusual in Colorado. But a number of other things *were* unusual.

"United Airlines, the other major carrier operating out of Denver, had canceled its Boise flights because of the storm."[1] Due to the United cancellations, Continental Flight 1713 was almost full. Undoubtedly, some of the passengers thought it unusual for one airline to cancel flights while another kept flying. But due to myriad unknown reasons and despite the severe weather, seventy-seven people boarded the plane.

Something else was highly unusual. Kelly Englehart, an experienced flight attendant, was concerned about the cockpit crew. "In an extraordinary step, she took Capt. Frank Zvonek aside at the gate and questioned him about the proficiency of the first officer. The man's extremely youthful appearance worried her."[2]

Her instincts, unfortunately, were on target.

> He was Lee Bruecher, 26, and in fact had completed his DC-9 flight training only eight weeks earlier and had hardly flown since. Before joining Continental, he had been fired from another job for his incompetence as a pilot. . . . Captain Zvonek told Kelly not to worry. He assured her that he would not let Bruecher land the plane on their return flight to Denver later that day. The prospect of the captain's letting the young first officer be at the controls during takeoff was so unthinkable to Kelly that it did not even occur to her to ask *that* question.

Yet the unusual continued to happen.

> As the DC-9 jetliner prepared for its roll down the runway . . . the captain was not at the controls. Instead, he had delegated primary flying duties to

First Officer Lee Bruecher. In addition to his dismal record with small commercial aircraft, Bruecher had spent only thirty-six hours in his whole life flying big commercial jet aircraft. And Frank Zvonek himself, the commander who had turned the controls over to Bruecher, had only thirty-three hours of experience as DC-9 captain. Neither man had ever flown a DC-9 in weather like this.

But one other irregular circumstance sealed the fate of Flight 1713.

Not only are pilots required to visually check the wings every twenty minutes during freezing wet weather, but no more than twenty minutes should elapse between de-icing and takeoff.

Particles of ice no larger than grains of coarse sandpaper can significantly disrupt the flow of air over the wing surface—a condition that has a critical effect on the plane's ability to lift during takeoff. On this day, twenty-seven minutes had elapsed since flight 1713 was de-iced—seven minutes beyond the maximum time—which gave ample opportunity for ice to form. Neither pilot ever emerged from the cockpit to walk back into the cabin and inspect the wing surfaces.[3]

What were they doing when they should have been checking the wings? According to the article,

The two Continental pilots had never met each other until this flight, but in the cockpit, after completing the standard checklists, they fell into a pattern of aimless chatter with sexual innuendoes about one of the female flight attendants. Their last thirty minutes of conversation, saved for posterity by the cockpit voice recorder, are more remindful of two adolescent boys on a camp-out than of two professionals charged with the safety of eighty men, women and children.[4]

The tragic outcome of these unusual circumstances? Flight 1713 crashed just seconds after takeoff, and twenty-eight people, including Zvonek and Bruecher, lost their lives.

You and I both know that competent teamwork in the cockpit of commercial airliners is the norm. That's why it's safer to fly than to drive. Yet this investigative report revealed an exception to that long-standing aviation tradition of teamwork between an experienced captain and copilot. There's a reason for two pilots up front: *two are better than one*. If the captain were to suffer a heart attack at thirty-two thousand feet, the first officer could safely bring the plane in. But there's another reason: one pilot can make a mistake. If one makes a mistake, chances are the other will notice and correct it.

The mistake made by the captain of Flight 1713 in failing to de-ice the plane within the given time limits should have been caught by the first officer. But it wasn't. And lives were lost because of the mutual error. It boiled down to a simple, yet catastrophic, lack of teamwork.

It's common to hear the phrase "It's amazing how quickly life flies by." I agree wholeheartedly. Life reminds me of flying a plane because life moves so incredibly fast. When the first edition of *Point Man* was published, I was forty years old. Now with this updated and revised edition, I'm seventy.

Where did those thirty years go? The answer is, they flew by.

That's why going through life with one's wife and kids reminds me of flying a plane. Not only does life fly by quickly, but as you and your wife go through each stage of life, you will find yourselves changing planes.

When you're in your thirties and forties (or even fifties) and your kids are young or in their teen years, life is not only fast, but it's also full—incredibly full. At that stage of life, you're not just flying any plane; you and your wife are flying a massive 747. When you get into your sixties and seventies, your life can still be very active, as long as the Lord grants you good health. But in my opinion, somewhere in your sixties, you start pulling your hamstring more often and find yourself having to slow down. Then you start downsizing, because you've got an empty nest and life isn't as nuts and crazy and full with constant activity and action as it was at age forty.

What I'm trying to say is that at some point you and your wife can trade in the 747. Who knows? By the time you hit seventy, maybe Elon Musk will have invented a two-person electric skateboard that will break the sound barrier and you'll be all set for the next stage of life.

But for now, if you're in your thirties, forties, or fifties with kids at home, you're flying the marriage 747. You and your wife are up front in the cockpit, trying to keep your ship airborne. You're surrounded by gauges, instruments, and lights. Everything is going smoothly . . . when suddenly a red light starts blinking furiously. That particular light indicates that your daughter needs braces—with a five-thousand-dollar price tag. A quick look at the financial gauge indicates that your dental account is close to empty. Your budget allowed for some cleanings and a few cavities but no braces. Where in the world will that money come from?

As you try to convince yourself that your daughter would look just fine with crooked teeth, the medical light indicates your five-year-old has just picked up mononucleosis from a kid at kindergarten. The pediatrician says that for him to fully recover, he is not to run, jump, or play for the next two years. Good luck.

Before you can work out the ramifications of keeping a five-year-old still for two years, an alarm goes off over your head. Your older son's favorite summer basketball camp has just raised its one-week fee from five hundred dollars to seventeen thousand dollars. The thought of hiring an arsonist to burn the camp down crosses your mind. But you can't do that. You're a Christian, remember?

Does any of this sound familiar? Of course it does. It's real life. It's tough trying to keep the family 747 in the air. That's why teamwork is as essential in the marriage cockpit as it is in a commercial jetliner.

How tragic that family 747s crash every day simply because husbands and wives fail to understand how they are to operate and function *as a team*. However, a couple that knows and practices the correct procedures greatly increases its chances of marital survival when the family airliner encounters sudden turbulence.

There are three necessary procedures that promote teamwork in the marriage cockpit:

- mutual understanding of the Romo-Witten principle
- mutual accountability
- mutual submission

If you can grab hold of these principles, not only will your wife appreciate you for it, but the chances of her following your leadership will increase dramatically.

MUTUAL UNDERSTANDING
OF THE ROMO-WITTEN PRINCIPLE

What version of the Bible do you prefer? The NIV, NASB, ESV, TLB, or NKJV? When it comes to Ephesians 5:22–23, I like the NFL version: "Tight ends, submit to your quarterback, as to the Lord. For the quarterback is the head of the tight ends as Christ is the head of the church."

This verse is the basis for what I call the Romo-Witten principle. Dallas Cowboys teammates Tony Romo and Jason Witten were one of the best passing combinations in the recent history of the NFL. To watch Romo and Witten operate was sheer bliss. Their ability to work together could shred an entire defense before you had a chance to finish swallowing your Gatorade.

The Romo-Witten principle has two components:

Component #1: Tony Romo had authority over Jason Witten.

Component #2: Jason Witten had to submit to Tony's authority.

Let's take a look at the significance of these two components. In the huddle, Romo made the decisions. When the play came in from the sideline, he was the one who decided whether or not to "audibilize" when at the line of scrimmage he saw the defense. The reason he could make these decisions is that he was the "head." That means he was the one with authority. In the huddle, Romo had the final say because he was the quarterback. Everyone on the team knew this. That's why when he audibilized, Jason didn't yell over to Tony and say, "That's the stupidest call I've ever heard in my life." Romo was the head, and he ultimately made the decisions on the field.

This doesn't mean that Witten was denied the opportunity to offer critical input into the decisions Romo made. If Witten came back to the huddle and told Romo that the linebacker kept taking his inside move and that he should fake to the inside and then run a post, Romo would listen to him. Why? Because they both had the same objective: to win.

Witten and the other Cowboys on the offensive unit "submitted" to Romo's leadership. The word translated *submit* in Ephesians 5:22 (NIV) means "to line one's self under." It was often used in the military sense of soldiers submitting to their superior. The word primarily has the idea of giving up one's own right or will.[5]

That's exactly what went on in the Cowboys' huddle. You had eleven strong-willed men with strong opinions. Yet for them to function as an effective unit, they chose to voluntarily give up their wills to follow the leadership of Romo.

Let me stress the fact that this principle does not inhibit or restrain good communication. Even though Witten was subject to Romo, he was still free to give his opinion. Because Romo was a good leader, he valued Witten's feedback. And the team as a whole submitted to Romo's leadership because they had learned to trust him.

The same principle applies to marriage. The real version of Ephesians 5:22–23 goes like this: "Wives, be subject to your *own husbands, as to the Lord. For the husband is the head of the wife, as Christ also is the head of the church.*"

One commentator made a very appropriate statement:

> To the wife it should be said that the form your submission takes will vary according to the quality of your husband's leadership. If the husband is a godly man who has a biblical vision for his family and leads out in the things of the Spirit, a godly woman will rejoice in this leadership and support him in it. You will no more be squelched by this leadership and support than the disciples were squelched by the leadership of Jesus.[6]

Did you catch that first sentence and the emphasis on the quality of the husband's leadership? It all goes back to trust. Trust is what motivates people to follow our leadership, whether at work or home. And trust must be earned.

Authority is not a bad idea. Without it, society would

spin off into anarchy. Edmund Burke once said, "An event has happened, upon which it is difficult to speak, and impossible to be silent."[7] Burke was referring to the impeachment of Warren Hastings, the governor-general of India, in 1789. In our day, male leadership in the home is a topic not easy to discuss but on which it's impossible to be silent, especially because the idea of the husband being head of the wife has come under such attack *within* the church.

Some scholars have gone to great lengths to insist that the word *head* doesn't carry with it ideas of authority. According to them, *head* means "source." I won't go into all the textual arguments on why there is a difference of opinion on the meaning of *head*. (See the appendix for more details on this issue.) But the significance of the discussion is this: if *head* doesn't mean authority, then God has not given to men the spiritual responsibility of leading their homes. Up until fifty years ago, that idea had never been seriously entertained in two thousand years of Christian scholarship.

The husband has been given authority in the home by God, just as the quarterback has it in the huddle and the captain has it in the cockpit. No question: male authority in the home is not a popular idea anymore. Maybe that's why the American family is in such trouble?

Scripture indicates that God holds the man responsible for decisions made in the family. One clear example is found in Genesis 3:1–13, when Adam and Eve were in the garden. The account plainly shows that it was Eve who first succumbed to temptation and brought sin into the world. Adam, unfortunately, soon repeated the disobedient act. Yet when God approached them to discuss the matter, *He purposely sought out Adam first*. It would have made more sense for Him to have approached Eve first, unless of course, by the man's headship position, he was ultimately accountable for those choices, just as the CEOs of corporations are ultimately responsible for the decisions made by their staffs.

Richard Wirthlin, who was President Ronald Reagan's pollster, told about the time he had to let his boss know his approval rating had fallen to a record low. The bad news came just one year after the assassination attempt, when Reagan's popularity had been at a record high.

Normally, Wirthlin didn't go in to see the president alone. This time no one went with him. Reagan took one look at the lone Wirthlin and said, "Tell me the bad news." Wirthlin told him. Not only had his approval rating dived since the assassination attempt, but it was the lowest approval rating of any president in his second year of office in the history of polls.

"'Dick . . . don't worry,' Reagan told him. 'I'll just go out there and try to get assassinated again.'"[8]

Perhaps my popularity rating with you has nose-dived with this perspective on male headship in the home. Many think the idea of male headship is out of touch and out of line. But before you assassinate my position, hear me out. I've found that what many people react to on this issue is not authority but the wrong use of authority. What they're reacting to is the idea of *authoritarianism*.

Authoritarianism is something we *should* react to, whether it occurs in an oppressed country or a Christian home.

A man has moved from proper authority to authoritarianism in his home when he demonstrates the following:

- He lacks interest in his wife's input and disregards her feelings.

- He forbids the children to discuss his decisions with him and is reluctant to let them make decisions on their own as they mature.
- He trusts few people.
- He displays an intense need to control those closest to him.

Authoritarianism is not ordained by God. But authority is. Authoritarianism didn't work in Eastern Europe, and it doesn't work on winning football teams or in effective homes.

In contrast to the "high control" authoritarian, the mature man who practices biblical headship is recognized by three characteristics:

- He loves his wife sacrificially.
- He loves his wife with understanding.
- He loves his wife with verbal praise.
- He encourages his wife to use her gifts.

A Mature Man Loves His Wife Sacrificially

A look at Ephesians 5:25 tells us that a husband's love is demonstrated by his willingness to sacrifice for his wife: "Husbands, love your wives, just as Christ also loved the church and gave Himself up for her."

But how does a wife measure the sacrificial love of her husband? For some reason, wives have the uncanny ability to measure our sacrificial love with the accuracy of a yardstick. They can recognize it from miles away. They intuitively know there is a direct correlation between service and sacrifice. And it usually comes out in the little things that spring from a right attitude.

A Mature Man Loves His Wife with Understanding

Most of us can identify with the apostle Peter. He was always putting his foot in his mouth or getting into some kind of difficulty. Peter was married. I'm sure that in the early years, like many of us, he was no prize to live with. He probably had much to learn about being a good husband. Toward the end of his life, as he had mellowed and matured, he wrote these words: "You husbands in the same way, live with your wives in an understanding way" (1 Peter 3:7).

The word *understanding* carries with it the idea of insight and tactfulness. No one enjoys being misunderstood. It's one of the truly miserable experiences in life. The woman who has a husband who knows when to put his arms around her and simply hold her close will inevitably feel understood. Sometimes that's the most insightful and tactful thing we can do. Don't offer a solution; just hold her.

I don't think that came easy for Peter; it certainly doesn't come naturally for me. But I'm learning. What is difficult for any wife, regardless of to whom she is married, is to be misunderstood. Peter knew that a woman who felt understood would have little difficulty following the leadership of a husband who led her in such an understanding way.

A Mature Man Loves His Wife with Verbal Praise

Peter gave us another piece of strategic advice when he wrote, "Show her honor as a fellow heir of the grace of life, so that your prayers will not be hindered" (1 Peter 3:7).

The word translated *honor* carries with it the idea of value. A mature man provides the kind of leadership to his wife that lets her know how valuable she is to him.

Verbal praise is a rare commodity in our world. That's why Mark Twain said, "I can live on a good compliment two weeks with nothing else to eat."[9] You may deeply appreciate your wife in your heart, but when was the last time you verbally expressed your appreciation to her? Perhaps you don't remember, but I would be willing to bet that *she* does.

There are severe consequences for the man who refuses to correct his errors with his wife. Peter puts it on the table. If you do not live with your wife in an understanding way and let her know she is valuable to you, your prayers will be hindered. That's how serious this is. You may be the most articulate man of prayer in your church, but if you are not implementing this scriptural prescription, you're wasting your breath. God will not respond.

The man who is careful not to miss his time of prayer yet neglects his wife's emotional needs fits the description that Daniel O'Connell gave of the British attorney Lord Manners: "He was the most sensible looking man talking nonsense I ever saw."[10]

A Mature Man Encourages His Wife to Use Her Gifts

Speaking of sense, what kind of man wouldn't encourage his wife in the area of her gifts? Why wouldn't he use his own time and resources to enable her to develop her gifts and flourish?

Answer: only the kind of man who is obsessed with himself and threatened by his wife's possible success.

When a man thinks a woman's only purpose is to serve him and make him look good, he is violating God's plan for marriage. Just as Jesus works constantly on our behalf to present us before the Father as mature and complete, you and I are to do the same for our wives. God gave her gifts for a reason, and your job is to help her discover that reason.

Mature leadership from a husband makes it easy for a wife to coexist in the marriage cockpit with him. A man who treats his wife with this kind of care and respect will do more than just coexist with her; they will both actually enjoy the ride.

MOVING BEYOND LEADERSHIP PARALYSIS

Leadership paralysis is a threat to male biblical leadership in the home.

This happens when a husband becomes passive and simply doesn't lead. Sometimes he hands over the leadership of his home to his wife; sometimes he just leaves a void, and his family ends up flying without anyone at the controls. This same man may be a strong leader at work, but when he walks in the door of his home, he takes off his leadership hat and withdraws or abdicates.

If your wife is always the one who makes sure the family goes to church, you are not leading spiritually. If she is handling the overall parenting decisions, you are not providing what your children need in a dad. Men have been endowed with certain traits that are rarely viewed as essential in our world. But God says they are essential. He tasks men with a specific role of leadership at home that women were never meant to fill. We are to set the course, and we will be held accountable for that. Guys, the buck stops with us.

There are many reasons why you (or any man) may have become passive at home:

- You may have had a terrible model or no model at all in your own dad, so you have no idea what a good leader looks like at home. A lack of preparation leads to a lack of confidence.

- You may be married to a strong woman who prefers to be in charge. Let's admit it: letting her call the shots and set the direction is just easier.
- Your wife may be a gifted leader; she may work in a position of leadership in a career; she may even make more money than you do. That certainly would give a man pause when it comes to leading her at home.
- You may work in a career that often takes you away from home, making it more difficult to lead.

When you get right down to it, every man has reason to feel unqualified. We all have weaknesses; we all have a lot to learn as we go. As the apostle James reminds us, "We all stumble in many ways" (3:2). But men and women have different strengths, and men have been designed by God for headship in the home. I have observed that even the strongest of women respect and appreciate men who are willing to step up to the plate and learn how to lead.

Spiritual leadership at home has nothing to do with income, personality, or special gifts. Spiritual leadership has everything to do with God's specific design of the man and His assignment from creation.

How does a man move out of passivity and into leadership? Here is a two-step strategy that will unlock paralysis:

1. Do the next right thing.
2. Understand that the next right thing will never violate Scripture. If it does, it's the next wrong step. So don't do it. Even if you're desperate. Obey the Lord and He will make a way. It's what He does. He's a Savior.

That's what men do. If there's confusion, you step into the void and initiate. If truth is needed, you speak up. If your wife needs protecting, you give her safety. If one of the children is out of control, you lovingly step in with boundaries. If prayer is needed, you bring the truth of Jesus by calling on His name: "Jesus, help us. We don't know what to do."

That's leadership.

I run into guys who tell me, "My wife and I are both Christians, but she has this job and she makes more money than I do. Doesn't she have authority because she brings in a higher income?" I say, "Well, actually, Scripture has nothing to say about salaries. You've been appointed, so this is how you need to function." Consider what happened at Apple when Steve Jobs went back for the second time. He was appointed to save the company but was paid only one dollar a year. However, there was no question that he was the appointed leader.

If your wife has been hurt by men in her past and feels threatened, be a different kind of man. Be patient and love her. When you mess up, be quick to ask for forgiveness. Lead her as Christ leads.

If I could define *headship* in a nutshell, I would put it this way: biblical headship for a husband is giving the best of all that he is to those under his care and authority. I would define *submission* in a complementary manner: biblical submission for a wife is giving the best of all she is to the one who is in authority over her.[11]

Several hundred years ago, Martin Luther described it this way: "Let the wife make the husband glad to come home, and let him make her sorry to see him leave." Or if you both work and you're working at home and she's coming home from her office, make her glad to see you and sad to go back to the office. You get it. If she stays home with the kids, the same principle applies. That is a high calling and the most difficult work of all. Whatever your situation is for now, follow the biblical plan: lead her intentionally, and honor her as a fellow heir in Christ. She will love you for that. That's good teamwork in anybody's book.

MUTUAL ACCOUNTABILITY

The poet Gerhard Frost once observed, "The reason mountain climbers are tied together is to keep the sane ones from going home."[12] That's what marriage is. It is two people tied together as they climb the mountain of life. They have to work as a team. They cannot work independently. To reach the summit, they must be interdependent. It takes teamwork to climb a mountain, to fly a 747, and to keep a marriage fresh and alive. It also takes mutual accountability.

Sometimes when a couple gets married, we'll say that they have "tied the knot." So they have . . . just like the mountain climbers who tie the knot to provide stability in case of a sudden blizzard or accident. Accountability is a protection for both parties.

Mutual accountability simply means that, as a husband, you explain your actions to her, and your wife explains hers to you. If mutual accountability had been practiced on Flight 1713, the flight might not have gone down.

The vast majority of men have wives who want their husbands to win. She is on his team. When a man begins to understand that, he views his wife in a new way. Your wife is a strategic gift to you! She has eyes that see what you don't, a mind that assimilates information from a different perspective, a heart with sensitivities you do not possess, and a personality with strengths that offset your weaknesses. That's built-in protection for you. It's why you must tap into her perspective as you lead your family. When she offers constructive criticism, learn to listen to her with an open mind.

Consider Her Perspective

Let's say a husband decides he wants to buy a new premium UHD smart TV with an eighty-two-inch flat screen. The mature husband realizes that such an item comes under the heading of a major purchase. He's looking at anywhere from two to four thousand bucks, minimum. Because it is a high-cost item, the mature husband will sit down with his wife to explain why he wants to get it, where the money is going to come from in the budget, and how the larger screen will keep him from going blind at an early age.

The mature husband realizes that his wife's perspective on the purchase is important. She may remind him that they recently discussed putting a new deck and patio in the backyard. There isn't money to purchase both the TV and the new addition to the backyard, and she thinks the latter is more important. As they discuss the issue, they will probably come to a decision both feel good about. And not only has a good decision been made, but they both know and understand the reasons behind it.

Contrast that process with the following scenario. On Saturday morning, the wife goes one direction to run errands, and the husband goes another to accomplish his list. When she gets home, he's sitting there watching the NCAA Final Four on his brand-new eighty-two-inch flat-screen smart TV that he picked up at Costco. "Got a *great* deal, honey!" To him, it's no biggie. Sometimes he buys new socks; sometimes he buys a new TV. As General Carl Spaatz said about one of his fellow officers, "He always thinks things over before he goes off half-cocked."[13]

Now, if this guy is head of his home, can he go out and make that kind of financial decision? Yes. Is that the wise way to make such a major purchase? No. The mature man makes himself mutually accountable to his wife by including her in the decision-making process. The immature man goes off and does what he wants without considering his wife's perspective. That is poor leadership no matter how you cut it. Eventually, such a man is going to make a major mistake because he isn't willing to explain his actions and process the feedback from his wife.

The Intimidation Factor

One way that some men keep from being mutually accountable is through intimidation.

This very problem can occur in marriage. An intimidating husband can become a control freak and run his home the way he wants. And he doesn't want suggestions from anyone—especially his wife. After all, he may think, according to the Scriptures, it's her "job" to submit to his authority.

This is one reason that Christian marriages are failing all over America. If a husband has a distorted view of what the Scriptures mean by "submission," he can intimidate his wife to the point that she will be afraid to speak up even when his leadership is clearly off base. He's getting ready to fly straight into the side of a mountain, but she's too afraid of how he'll react if she says something.

We need to get one thing straight: submission is not just an issue for wives. Yes, Ephesians 5:22 does say, "Wives, be subject to your own husbands." But submission is a responsibility that applies to every one of us. Submission is inescapable and universal. Everyone submits.

A young sentry, on guard duty for the first time, had orders not to admit any car unless it had a special identification seal. The first unmarked car the sentry stopped contained a general. When the general told his driver to go right on through, the sentry politely said, "I'm new at this, sir. Who do I shoot first, you or the driver?"

The sentry had it right. Everybody submits. Submission is for generals, presidents, teachers, students, accountants, attorneys, Central American dictators, and wives. It's also for husbands. No one escapes submission. We are all under authority.

Scripture gives several examples:

- Spiritual leaders have authority over a church congregation (see Hebrews 13:17).
- Governing authorities (elected officials, police officers, and so on) have authority over citizens (see Romans 13:1).
- Husbands have authority in the home (see Ephesians 5:22).
- Parents have authority over their children (see Ephesians 6:1).
- Children have authority over their pets—no kidding! (see Genesis 1:28).

Let's face it. None of us like the idea of submitting to someone else. The classic American phrase is "No one's going to tell *me* what to do!"

I believe Scripture teaches that the husband is the head of the marriage relationship and that the wife is ultimately to submit to his authority. But I also believe that a man should not demand submission from his wife. Instead, he should be such an exemplary model of submission to the authorities in his own life that he provides the kind of leadership at home that is easy to follow.

Mutual submission simply means that you each consider the other person over yourself. There is a good reason that Paul began this whole passage on husband/wife relationships with the command to "submit to one another out of reverence for Christ" (Ephesians 5:21, NIV). Many a man has camped on verses 22–24 without ever noticing the context. Submission is not an issue just for wives; it is a Christian issue that affects every member of the body of Christ.

For me, the best example of mutual submission is watching a great basketball team like the Golden State Warriors. The best teams are made up of players who practice this principle of submission. When Draymond Green set a screen so that Klay Thompson could get open to take a pass from Stephen Curry, that was mutual submission at work. There were five guys playing, but only one guy could take the shot. So Green submitted by setting a screen, Curry submitted by passing instead of shooting, and Thompson submitted by following his missed shot, getting the rebound, and dishing it off to DeMarcus Cousins—who jammed it in for two.

If you followed the Warriors over an entire season, you'd

notice that in one game Thompson would be the high scorer, another night Kevin Durant, then Curry, then Thompson, then Durant, and so on. In other words, in any given game they would go with the guy who had the hot hand. That was mutual submission. Each player wanted to win and was willing to "place himself under" to get the victory.

Mutual submission *does not* mean that the husband and wife take turns being the head of the home. That is the man's permanent assignment. It does mean that the husband demonstrates and models the concept of submission in his own life when the situation calls for such a response. Mutual submission is just another way of describing servant leadership for the husband and loving submission for the wife. *It is at the core of both biblical headship and biblical submission.*

"JUST AS"

We've said quite a bit about the principles that make for good teamwork in marriage. Maybe I've said too much. If this seems like a lot to absorb, let me bottom-line it for you. There are only two words a man has to remember about leading his wife: *just as*.

If you can't recall anything else in this chapter, remember those two words and you'll have it all. In Ephesians 5:25, Paul wrote, "Husbands, love your wives, *just as* Christ also loved the church and gave Himself up for her."

In other words, if you are not sure how to lead or how to respond in a given situation, take your cue from Christ and do it *just as* He loved the church. Christ is our role model for loving our wives.

Back in the eighties, Steve DeVore built a multimillion-dollar company on the principle of role modeling. DeVore was president of SyberVision, a company that marketed instructional video- and audiotapes on everything from golf to skiing to weight control. This was not some kind of mystical New Age approach to learning but rather the master-apprentice relationship put to work in different settings.

When DeVore was in college, he happened to watch a bowling tournament on TV. As he paid close attention to the movements of the bowlers, the thought struck him that if he could emulate their movements, he could probably achieve the same results.

After watching the bowlers closely for thirty minutes, he got in his car and drove to the local bowling alley. He got a lane, picked out a ball, and for the next thirty minutes did *just as* the professional bowlers had done on TV. He threw nine straight strikes and recorded a score of 278. His highest score prior to that point was 163. By emulating a proficient role model, he improved his performance by 115 pins. But the key was *just as*. He had to do it *just as* the pros.

Men, if we will pay close attention to the methods of Jesus Christ, we can fly our marriage 747s with more harmony and satisfaction in the cockpit than we ever thought possible.

If you need more guidance, check in with your Lord in the control tower. His calm voice can guide you and your co-captain through the darkest of nights to a perfect landing . . . *together.*

7

RESTORING THE ANCIENT BOUNDARIES OF GENDER AND MARRIAGE

Serve Christ, back him; let his cause be your cause; give not an hairbreadth of truth away; for it is not yours, but God's.

—Samuel Rutherford

John Trapp, the wise and profound pastor, once wrote that "truth must be spoken, however it be taken."[1] Here is a Scripture verse that in our current culture has not been taken very well: "God created man in His own image, in the image of God He created him; male and female He created them" (Genesis 1:27). For thousands of years, there was not even a hint of controversy about that verse. Those days are over.

My longtime friend Stu Weber demonstrated the utmost importance of this verse for a generation that is utterly confused:

> Masculinity did not evolve. It was *created*. . . . Gender is one of the most basic and far-reaching expressions of the image of God. . . . God created mankind "in His image . . . male and female He created them." The image and glory of God on this planet is tied to our human masculinity and femininity. . . . To tinker with the image of God, represented in male and female, is to slap God in the face.[2]

Understand this. In these days, God is being slapped in the face, and the sexual identity of our kids is being destroyed on a daily basis—all by the deception of the enemy.

You remember the enemy's other strategies for destroying your family? The first is to alienate and sever your relationship with your wife. The second is to alienate and sever your relationship with your children.

That's where we are today as I write this chapter in 2021. Satan wants to drive an impenetrable wedge between you and your children. The last thing he cares about is your kids' happiness and well-being. He wants to steal them away and ultimately destroy them. And today one of his primary tactics is gender deception and lies.

A child's sexuality is at the very core of his identity. Confuse his sexuality and you have turned his world upside down.

In the past ten years, the enemy has led a shock-and-awe

campaign the likes of which you and I never could have imagined just a few years earlier. Christian men have been caught off guard. His strategy has been to create a tectonic shift in our cultural belief system about human sexuality. He has harnessed our media and entertainment, educational system, legislators, policy makers, courts (including the highest court of our land), and, yes, certain church thinkers and leaders. They have bought into the lies of Satan and rejected the truth of God.

C. S. Lewis was a brilliant writer and observer of culture. Years ago, he wrote these words: "The most dangerous ideas in a society are not the ones being argued, but the ones that are assumed."[3] In our culture right now, two things are being assumed and they both are lies from the enemy.

First, *gender is not fixed; it is fluid.*

Second, *marriage is not restricted to one man and one woman.*

These lies are the new assumptions, and the secular elites want to force them down your throat.

The blows have been swift and overwhelming. They've come from every corner. We are hit by a Supreme Court ruling on gay marriage, but before we can get our bearings, lawsuits based on that ruling are filed against bakers and Christian adoption agencies. But before we can process the implications of that, we learn about public school K–12 curriculum being developed promoting LGBTQ choices as normal and good. But before we can get on top of that, we find out that in some states, a child can be dropped off at school and secretly identify as a different gender and name of his or her choosing—with the mandated support of teachers and without parents ever knowing. But before we can wrap our minds around this, we read about a Christian leader who has left his wife and kids and joined the LGBTQ lifestyle.

Suddenly we are considered by friends and family to be harsh and unloving for holding to Scripture. And even though we'd be doing it out of love, we dare not recommend a book that helps parents to raise masculine sons and feminine daughters. No one wants to become a social pariah. That's the enemy's strategy: hit, confuse, intimidate, alienate, and neutralize.

He wants us shell shocked.

Satan knows that a father and mother are the key to a little child's stable sexual identity, so his number one goal is to disorient and neutralize us. If he can do that, he can eliminate our influence, separate out our children, and pick them off one by one.

We must take hold of every spiritual weapon and resource the Lord has provided to fight this battle. Whatever you do, you can't put it in neutral. You must get involved and be aggressive.

I'll be honest with you. In all my years of writing to men (and there have been some twenty books since I first wrote *Point Man*), I have never faced the spiritual resistance I've encountered in writing this updated chapter. *Never.* In the past year, I have read dozens of books and started numerous drafts, only to find myself at a loss as to how to tackle this task. More than once I came close to losing heart and walking away from it. But I knew I couldn't do that. There is just too much at stake.

We must be strong in the Lord and in the strength of His might. And we must know that the battle is His.

It's important we keep the biblical facts on the front burners of our minds. Satan is not all-powerful. "Greater is He who is in you than he who is in the world" (1 John 4:4). The stakes are high, but the battle eventually will be won. God will navigate us through the lies and deceptions of the evil one as we put on the spiritual armor and rely on the sword of the Spirit, which is the Word of God (see Ephesians 6:10–17).

Let me remind you of something else. You are not called to save the whole world. That's our Lord's job. You're called to focus on your sons and daughters. Is the issue complex and overwhelming? If we look at only our world, it will be. You and I can get tied in knots over it. But here's the truth. Contrary to what Satan would have you believe, your job is not complex. It is clear and straightforward.

What is your job? *It is to restore the ancient boundaries in your family even as the enemy continues to remove them.*

THE ANCIENT BOUNDARIES OF GOLF

Several years ago, I read about a young woman by the name of Lexi Thompson. She was apparently an excellent golfer on the Ladies Professional Golf Association circuit and was leading in a tournament by two strokes. The match was on national TV, and it was Sunday, the last day. She was on her way to the thirteenth green. As she was lining up her putt, an official walked over and took her aside. He explained that a TV viewer had sent in an email saying that on the previous day, when she picked up her ball and marked it, she had replaced it an inch from the original mark. After reviewing the play, the officials agreed. In keeping with the rules of golf, they were now assessing her a four-stroke penalty. Needless to say, she didn't go on to win the tournament.

This shocking penalty was unprecedented—that one viewer

somewhere in TV land would have that kind of influence is somewhat astonishing. But I will say this for golf: they've set the ancient boundaries and they will not be moved.

Tragically, we are living in a day when we are very careful about the boundaries of golf but very careless about the boundaries that affect our souls.

You can't live life without boundaries. There are property boundaries, as stated in Proverbs 22:28: "Do not move the ancient boundary which your fathers have set." God distributed the land to the twelve tribes, and boundaries were put in place and property lines carefully drawn. That's still true today. If a neighbor comes over to your property and cuts down your tree because he's short on firewood, that's a violation of an important boundary.

The Ten Commandments are moral boundaries that God, out of His holiness, drew for all generations. They are for our good.

There are certain boundaries you don't mess with—ever. As a Christian man, you acknowledge that God drew two boundary lines back in Genesis when He created the heavens and the earth. These are not property boundaries; they are moral boundaries from the very character of God Almighty.

We call them "ancient" because they were laid down when God created the world. That's about as ancient as it gets. These two boundaries are for all people for all time. And they are not to be moved. They may be ancient, but they are always relevant. God's moral law has no expiration date.

The first ancient boundary is that *gender is fixed*.

The second ancient boundary is that *marriage is between only a man and a woman*.

These boundaries are the foundation of civilization. When they are abandoned, without exception that civilization will go down. (Read Romans 1:18–32 for a blow-by-blow description.)

Satan detests these boundaries. So he systematically removes them.

I was caught one night in a blizzard at the Minneapolis–Saint Paul International Airport, and of course I was disappointed by the delay. But then I saw a regiment of huge snowplows working in stunning synchronization, like a marching band, sweeping away the rapidly accumulating snowdrifts on the runways. They cleared those runways, and before I knew it, I was on a plane and we were taking off.

In our times, there is a cultural regiment of snowplows that is utterly dedicated to clearing away the ancient boundaries of gender and marriage. Our children are being taught that gender is fluid and that marriage is not restricted to a man and woman. Everywhere they turn they are learning that these ideas are normal and good; the ideas are "progressive"; they are to be "celebrated."

Our Lord gives this warning:

Woe to those who call evil good, and good evil;
Who substitute darkness for light and light for darkness;
Who substitute bitter for sweet and sweet for bitter!
Woe to those who are wise in their own eyes
And clever in their own sight! (Isaiah 5:20–21)

Know this: these notions being passed off as good and natural and beautiful to our children are, in actuality, evil. They are dark and bitter. The further you get away from God and the further you get away from His boundaries, the more people are hurt, the more people are wounded, and the more families are broken up. The more grief, the more pain, and the more tragedy you invite into your life.

Boundaries are the guardrails on the path of life. I'm talking about *life* in the fullest sense—physical, emotional, mental, psychological, and spiritual. God's boundaries protect us. They prevent us from losing our way. They keep us from plunging headlong into a dark and dangerous world. Proverbs 16:25 says, "There is a way which seems right to a man, but its end is the way of death."

And here's more insight from Scripture:

> Know therefore today, and take it to your heart, that the LORD, He is God in heaven above and on the earth below; there is no other. So you shall keep His statutes and His commandments which I am giving you today, that it may go well with you and with your children after you. (Deuteronomy 4:39–40)

The Lord is greatly concerned with the well-being of our children and grandchildren. He loves them more than we do. He is all-wise. He is supremely good. He tells us the truth.

You've probably heard that the way to recognize a counterfeit bill is to study the real thing. Here's another one for you: if you want to catch Satan in a lie, get God's truth etched in your brain. What is the truth about human sexuality? You don't have to read twenty books to figure it out. You just need to read Genesis 1 and 2.

The Creator's Plan

God set the boundary of gender in Genesis 1:27: "God created man in His own image, in the image of God He created him; *male and female* He created them."

God set the boundary of marriage in Genesis 2:24: "A man shall leave his father and his mother, and be joined to his wife; and they shall become one flesh."

Jesus affirmed these boundaries in Mark 10. The Pharisees were always trying to trip up our Lord, but they never came close, because it's extremely difficult to trip up God. He completely turned the tables on them by tying together these two boundaries of gender and marriage. This is a big deal, because we have a growing, professing-Christian subculture that wants to speak highly of Jesus while moving the boundaries. If Jesus affirmed the boundaries, then so should His men and women.

The Pharisees were asking Him a trick question about divorce and what Moses taught. Pay close attention to how Jesus handled these guys, starting in verse 6. They raised the issue of divorce when that was not the issue. The issue was the ancient boundaries:

> From the beginning of creation, God made them male and female. For this reason a man shall leave his father and mother, and the two shall become one flesh; so they are no longer two, but one flesh. What therefore God has joined together, let no man separate. (verses 6–9)

Jesus took them back to creation and the two ancient boundaries.

By the way, how would Jesus know this? Well, obviously

He read it. But there's another reason He knows this. *He was there* at creation. He is the eternal God and—don't miss this—He was also the Creator. Jesus created male and female. He instituted the ordinance of marriage. John tells us that "all things came into being through Him, and apart from Him nothing came into being that has come into being" (John 1:3). Colossians says it again in 1:16: "By Him all things were created."

Jesus existed in the beginning, and He created male and female. So as the God-Man, in Mark 10:6–9, He was rehearsing the importance of God's design in gender found in Genesis 1: "From the beginning of creation, God made them male and female."

Then He moved on to God's design for marriage, found in Genesis 2:

> For this reason a man shall leave his father and mother, and the two shall become one flesh; so they are no longer two, but one flesh. What therefore God has joined together, let no man separate.

We often hear these words at weddings. Why? We are acknowledging the ancient boundaries that were fixed and reaffirmed by Jesus Christ. Old Testament scholar Derek Kidner explained that when Jesus coupled *male* and *female* (see Genesis 1:27) with *marriage* (see 2:24), He was establishing the "twin pillars of marriage."[4]

So there it is, guys. This isn't rocket science. God's plan for marriage is crystal clear: one man, one woman, united together, never to separate. Oh, and when they marry, that's when they have sex. I probably didn't have to spell that one out for you. Or come to think of it, maybe I did. Our culture tends to think that unhindered sexual experimentation and coupling with numerous partners should begin right about the time a kid gets a driver's permit. That was not and is not God's plan (see 1 Thessalonians 4:1–8).

God gave the woman to the man to be his counterpart. Male and female He chiseled them. He created them to fit. He gave them, together, dominion over the earth to be wise stewards of its resources. And He commanded them to have children. A man with a man cannot have children. A woman with a woman cannot have children. The sexual bond between man and wife is to be exclusive, it's to be permanent, and they are to produce offspring.

John Stonestreet put it simply: "The natural family is built around the biological realities of male and female and procreation, and it's therefore as irreplaceable as gravity."[5]

Read carefully this summation by Peter Sprigg of the Family Research Council:

> The most important thing for Christian parents to communicate to their children about this issue is that God created each of us either male or female, as it says in Genesis 1:27. . . . This short but profound verse implies several things.
>
> 1) Our "maleness" and "femaleness" is an essential part of our humanity as God created us;
> 2) *It is good to be male,* and *it is good to be female,* because in either case, we bear the image of God; and

3) *We have neither the right nor the power to change the sex (male or female) that God has given us,* because it is part of his created order.[6]

God's ancient boundaries draw a clear line between His design and the lesbian, gay, bisexual, transgender, queer, or any other "plus" of the LGBTQ movement sweeping our nation and bringing so much destruction.

Some people say that's pretty strict. But I didn't come up with it! Jesus did. Jesus tells us the truth. And the truth sets us free.

A professing Christian has to do some neck-breaking contortions and gymnastics to come up with anything else. And believe me, it is being attempted. The problem is, you have to ignore the whole of Scripture in order to land anywhere else. Passage after passage underscores the ancient boundaries.[7] When scriptures are systematically rationalized away, slowly but surely the Bible loses authority. And when the Bible has no authority, what then? It's anyone's guess. Who's to say what is and isn't true?

We don't stand over the Bible and edit it to fit what we want. We get under the Bible because it is the ultimate authority from God Almighty. We obey Him by obeying His book. We slide into sexual chaos when we try to make ourselves the authority over the Bible. That's precisely why dry rot has set into our nation and our lives.

Removing the Boundaries

Go with me back to the fall of 2019. I've just gotten home from a Wednesday night men's Bible study. I'm worn out and I'm looking for a basketball game on TV. I'm just flipping through the channels, trying to find the right one, and I come across HGTV. Another couple is looking for a home. I stop for a minute to learn what kind of home they are looking for. Maybe they should buy *my* home?

It's fascinating to watch, though it's always pretty much the same. They're going to buy a house, and they have three options. "Are they going to get the Cape Cod or go with the modern one? And then there's the log cabin that's off the grid and has a remodeled outhouse. Oh my gosh, what are they going to do? She wants that one, and he wants the other one. How are they going to work this out? I mean, this is huge!"

But, actually, it's boring after a couple of minutes, and I continue my flipping journey through 286 channels. Twenty minutes later, I'm completing my lap and I arrive back at HGTV, and it's a new couple. I guess the other couple got it worked out and are now living happily ever after.

But this new "couple" woke me out of my stupor. There were three people standing in the kitchen instead of two. It's a husband and wife who have a ten-year-old and twelve-year-old, and I thought the second woman was the nanny. I'm just about to flip the channel, when the husband says, "My wife is bisexual, and we are in a throuple relationship." A throuple is three people. They were buying a house in Colorado Springs, and it was on HGTV just like they were baking chocolate chip cookies. No big deal—but actually it's a big deal. I've just witnessed another ancient boundary being toppled like a statue in the town square.

Fifty years ago, your grandparents lived in a world held together by the ancient boundaries. Yet today, we've gone from couples to throuples. How did we slip away so far, so quickly?

An avalanche starts long before the slide. Not even a satellite can see it in the making. From above it looks like any old snow on any old mountain. But give it a few days or weeks of snow, rain, and temperature changes, and you'll get a buildup of an invisible, unstable snowpack. When that snowpack can't take the increasing weight of snow anymore, it breaks free and tears down the mountainside. In the blink of an eye, it accelerates and picks up anything along the way.

Our sexual avalanche did not start with homosexuality. It started long ago with the acceptance of no-fault divorce, cohabitation, and nonmarital births. This was the growing snowpack that was about to break free.

By the late twentieth century, we were urged as a society to forget biology and DNA and buy into the idea that there is a gay gene. Was that gene ever found? No. But it was a brilliant sleight of hand, attempting to explain same-sex attraction as inborn:

> The American Psychological Association (APA), which is gay affirming, recognizes the lack of scientific evidence for the claim that homosexuality is genetic: "Although much research has examined the possible genetic, hormonal, developmental, social and cultural influences on sexual orientation, no findings have emerged that permit scientists to conclude that sexual orientation is determined by any particular factor or factors."[8]

Even gay-rights activist Martin Duberman, founder of the Center for LGBTQ Studies (CLAGS) at the City University of New York, agrees: "No good scientific work establishes that people are born gay or straight."[9]

Oddly, the same-sex camp came into conflict with itself:

some claimed gays could not help themselves; others claimed that no, it was a choice. We were confused by the flurry of "experts." There was this study and that, this expert opinion and that. But no matter. *Romantic, sexual attraction was the key.*

A full-court press was on to overwhelm us with the lie. Eventually, the DSM (Diagnostic and Statistical Manual of Mental Disorders) for the American Psychiatric Association changed the category of homosexuality from abnormal to normal sexual behavior. And, well, in the world at large, that was the end of it. It is now considered normal for a man to be born a male, with a penis and all the other physiological paraphernalia, but actually be an emotional and sexual female. A woman could be born a woman, with a vagina and all the other physiological paraphernalia, but actually be an emotional and sexual male.

The snowpack had broken loose and was now hurtling down our cultural landscape.

Why, then, should a man not be able to have sex with another man, or a woman with another woman? And so it went. If the basis of a relationship is sexual attraction, why should those who identify as homosexual not be able to have multiple partners? Don't heterosexuals? And if same-sex relationships are okay, why should these be prevented from marriage?

Since the normalizing of homosexuality, our sexual avalanche has picked up astonishing momentum.

Ryan Anderson and Robert George are world-class scholars and committed Christians. Anderson is head of the Witherspoon Institute. George is a professor at Princeton. They wrote an opinion article in *USA Today* called "Decade in Review: Marital Norms Erode," in which they outlined the different court cases that quickly avalanched us from one-man/one-woman marriage to same-sex marriage. All of that happened in just ten years. The ancient boundary of marriage was taken out.[10]

You know about polyamory, right? That's the practice of having sexual relationships with multiple people with the consent of all people involved. The Polyamory Society defines it as "the nonpossessive, honest, responsible, and ethical philosophy and practice of loving multiple people simultaneously. . . . Polyamory emphasizes consciously choosing how many partners one wishes to be involved with rather than accepting social norms which dictate loving only one person at a time."[11]

Nonpossessive. Honest. Responsible. Ethical. Loving. Freeing. From what? From ancient "dictates." The enemy propaganda is staggering. Remember the throuple on HGTV and their two adolescent children? You think those children are not being indoctrinated?

Let's stop for a minute and think about where we are. Just ten years ago, the vast majority of Americans agreed with the ancient boundaries. But the avalanche has gone over the cliff. We are in free fall, completely untethered to God's sane and good plan in Genesis. That's why a Gallup poll recently reported that "Americans see divorce, fornication, gay relations as more morally acceptable than wearing fur."[12]

That's insane.

I find it very interesting that God gave the animals to the man and woman so that after they sinned in Genesis 3, they could wear fur, while at the same time He forbade divorce, fornication, and gay relations.

We need to slice through all this enemy propaganda. And 1 Corinthians 6 does just that:

Do you not know that the unrighteous will not inherit the kingdom of God? *Do not be deceived;* neither fornicators, nor idolaters, nor adulterers, nor effeminate [referring to the passive recipient in a homosexual relationship], nor homosexuals, nor thieves, nor the covetous, nor drunkards, nor revilers, nor swindlers, will inherit the kingdom of God. *Such were some of you;* but you were washed, but you were sanctified, but you were justified in the name of the Lord Jesus Christ and in the Spirit of our God. (verses 9–11)

Homosexuality is not genetic, because, in fact, there were some who were in a lifestyle of homosexuality and then Jesus got hold of them.

If you're a shoplifter, it's not genetic. If you're a liar, it's not a gene. It's a sinful heart and a sinful nature. Such *were* some of you. But you were washed, sanctified, and justified. Because of Jesus Christ, you no more are these things (fornicators, idolaters, adulterers, effeminate, homosexuals, thieves, and so on). You have been saved from those behaviors and identities. Jesus changes lives. He sets you on a path of grace and growth.

Does this mean that all men look alike? In other words, are all boys supposed to be rough and tumble? Absolutely not. Some boys are sensitive by nature; they prefer the arts or sitting in a corner with a book. These boys are still very much uniquely male in their God-given DNA.

What about women? Do all little girls love wearing dresses and twirling about the room like a ballerina? Of course not. Some girls aren't girlie girls; they're athletic, they're initiative takers, and they're leaders by nature. But they're still very much uniquely female in their God-given DNA.

Let us not be deceived. Homosexuality is a perversion of God's plan.

The Transgender Tragedy

You know that point in an avalanche where an unsuspecting person is caught up by the power of the moving snow and buried alive? Well, that was Walt Heyer. Only by the grace of Jesus Christ did he survive the avalanche of transgenderism that buried him. One of the books he has written is called *Trans Life Survivors*. And his story is powerful.

When Walt was a little boy, his parents were busy, so he ended up spending a lot of time with his grandmother. As you would expect, he bonded with her. Every time he was with her, she put him in a dress. *Every time.* She would fix him up as a girl; a little lipstick, a little rouge, little earrings, all of that. His parents knew nothing of this. "My grandmother only affirmed me as a girl, never as a boy," says Walt. "How pretty I looked, how feminine! 'Oh, you walk so sweetly. Oh, you're such a beautiful girl.'" This went on for two and a half years. When his father found out, he was livid. The result was greater distance between Walt and his dad, which only compounded his growing confusion over his male identity.

Walt grew up to be extremely successful and wealthy. He was a brilliant engineer and a gifted leader. He worked as a design engineer with NASA, then became a corporate executive with one of the top-selling car companies in America. He married and had kids, went to a Bible-believing church, and in the summer would take his kids to a Bible camp that I've spoken at in California. But inwardly he was plagued by what had happened to him as a little kid. He began a secret life of frequenting gay bars and cross-dressing. He never cared about homosexuality, but in the Tenderloin area of San Francisco, he could cross-dress freely and carry on as a woman. He became obsessed with finding his true identity. Was he really a woman living in a man's body? He went from psychiatrist to psychiatrist, looking for answers. Doctors convinced him he had gender dysphoria and that the answer was sexual reassignment.

In his midforties, he made the decision. He found a team of doctors in Colorado who began the process of gender reassignment and gave him the surgery in 1983. For eight years he lived as a woman named Laura. But it wasn't the answer he had been searching for. The surgery had not changed anything in his life. In fact, he was more tortured than ever before, and the hopelessness was overwhelming.

One day he walked into a church that my brother Jeff pastored in California. He began attending as Laura, a middle-aged single woman who attended women's retreats, Bible studies, and church services and was just there—a faithful part of the church. Several months in, Laura called Jeff and went in for an appointment. She sat down and said, "Jeff, I need to tell you something. My name is not Laura. My name is Walt."

Well, that may have been one of the most unforgettable moments in Jeff's counseling history. Walt began to tell Jeff his story and how he came to recognize that only Christ could put his life together. "What I've realized is that I have been utterly deceived. Nothing has changed in my life. In fact, my life has gotten worse. What I'm coming to realize, and I have been studying psychology over at UC Santa Cruz over the last year, is that there are issues from my background as a kid that I've never resolved. That's what I need to work on. But God is calling me to detransition from a woman back to a man. I don't know what to do."[13]

Jeff said, "I don't know what to do either, but I bet the Lord will help us walk through it. I'm sure glad you're here."

They began the process. Months later at a morning service, Jeff went up to the pulpit with Laura and they told the story. They explained that Laura was going back to being Walt. (By the way, two other churches—prior to Walt's coming to my brother's church—would have nothing to do with him. They didn't want him around. They didn't know what to do with him. But in Jeff's church he was embraced and loved.) The Lord started to heal Walt's heart, and those issues from his background began to be dealt with. It was not an easy road, but he became Walt again and has an amazing testimony of God's grace and a remarkable ministry helping others who are struggling as he once was. As Walt put it, "My story testifies to the truth that we must never give up on people, no matter how many times they fail or how long recovery takes. We must never underestimate the healing power of prayer and love in the hands of the Lord. We must never give up hope."[14]

I recently talked to Walt, who is now (in 2020) eighty years old. He gets up at around 4:00 a.m., grabs his coffee, reads his Bible, spends time in prayer, and then answers emails from people all over the world who have heard his testimony or read his books. People reach out to him because they know he understands what they're going through. He was deceived as they have been deceived. His life was destroyed as their lives have been destroyed. And they are crying out for help. "Don't take your life," he tells them.

"Don't take your life. Christ can heal you. Christ can put you back together."

Walt also tells them that "the LORD is near to the broken-hearted and saves those who are crushed in spirit" (Psalm 34:18).

A 2011 study in Sweden followed 324 people who had sex-reassignment surgery (191 male-to-females, 133 female-to-males) from 1973 to 2003. The overall rate of death was higher than expected, with suicide being the leading cause. Those who had the sex-change surgery were almost twenty times more likely to take their own life than the non-transgender population. They were also more likely to seek inpatient treatment for psychiatric conditions.[15]

By God's grace, Walt discovered the ancient truth that God created him to be a man. And all the treatments and surgeries in the world would never change his God-given DNA. He didn't need surgery. He needed a Savior. (You can learn more about Walt at his website, WaltHeyer.com.)

Abigail Shrier, author of *Irreversible Damage*, wrote,

> Until just a few years ago, "gender dysphoria"—severe discomfort in one's biological sex—was vanishingly rare. It was typically found in .01 percent of the population, emerged in early childhood, and afflicted males almost exclusively.
>
> But today whole groups of female friends in colleges, high schools, and even middle schools across the country are coming out as "transgender." These are girls who had never experienced any discomfort in their biological sex until they heard a coming-out story from a speaker at a school assembly or discovered the internet community of trans "influencers."

Unsuspecting parents are awakening to find their daughters in thrall to hip trans YouTube stars and "gender-affirming" educators and therapists who push life-changing interventions on young girls—including medically unnecessary double mastectomies and puberty blockers that can cause permanent infertility.[16]

Cari Stella is one of many voices of this younger generation coming out with warnings about the great transgender lie. I came across her story on the website for *World* magazine:

When Cari Stella recounts her transgender experience in a series of YouTube videos, she doesn't shed tears, but she does talk about pain.

As a teenage girl, Stella felt a strong desire to live as a man. A therapist obliged. After three or four visits over a three-month period, and without suggesting other options, the therapist prescribed testosterone. Stella was 17. A few years later, she underwent a double mastectomy.

Stella says her family was supportive, and her workplace included transgender leadership. Her transition seemed like a success. Except it wasn't.

Soon, Stella says, she felt worse, not better. It took a while, but she says testosterone "made me even more dissociated" than she felt when she started. It was "hard to figure out that the treatment you're being told is to help you is actually making your mental health worse."

After three years of hormones, Stella stopped taking testosterone and detransitioned to living as a woman. She's still grappling with the effects of her ordeal: "I'm a real, live 22-year-old woman with a scarred chest and a broken voice and 5 o'clock shadow because I couldn't face the idea of growing up to be a woman."

Eventually she realized, "I could not continue running from myself."[17]

Today, gender dysphoria dominates the discussion of sexuality. Transgenderism is replacing the once debated issue of homosexuality. And preadolescent children are becoming the target.

Tony Perkins of the Family Research Council recently wrote about the concerted campaign to reach preadolescent children. It's happening in states across America, including California, Michigan, and Wisconsin. If you live in Madison, Wisconsin, for example, once you drop your children off at school and they walk through the school doors, they can identify as another gender without your knowledge. They will be referred to by the new name of their choice, they will change bathrooms, and by bureaucratic fiat, teachers are told not to inform the parents. In parent-teacher meetings, the children will be referred to by their name at home. But at school, they go back to their new identity. It's stunning. Your kid can even get sex-hormone therapy without your knowing. They can't have Advil without your permission, but they can start hormone therapy.[18]

This is such tragic, heavy stuff. But every parent needs to know that there's an agenda. The transgender lobby is huge; it has weaponized our media, our political halls of power, our universities, and our medical communities. How many doctors and professors and psychologists are being driven out because they hold to the ancient boundaries? How many children are being separated out and tragically picked off?

Many studies (such as those done by Vanderbilt University and London's Portman Clinic) have shown that the majority of children who report transgender feelings spontaneously lose those feelings.[19]

If I could recommend one book (and there are many) to help you raise your children well even in this toxic environment, it would be *Gender Ideology: What Do Christians Need to Know?* by Dr. Sharon James.[20] She has a PhD from Cambridge and is in ministry in England with her husband, who is principal of the London Seminary. The book is only about a hundred pages. It's clear, biblical, compassionate, truthful, and balanced.

Dr. James wrote,

> Parents should remember that there's a totally natural and completely safe way of resolving childhood gender confusion. It's called puberty. When children do genuinely experience discontent with their biological sex, if puberty is allowed to take its natural course—and you allow the testosterone to kick in for boys, estrogen for girls—in the vast majority of cases, gender confusion is resolved. Children and young people are impressionable and immature. We don't allow them to make big decisions in other areas.[21]

Fundamentally, according to Dr. James, *gender confusion involves deep unhappiness.*[22]

If gender discontent and confusion persist, look for the deep unhappiness. Ask the Lord to help you get to the root of it. As you attempt to shepherd your children through the chaos around them, ask the Lord to shepherd and lead you too.

A FATHER'S MISSION

I recently saw a professional athlete and his wife being interviewed. They'd been in the media limelight a lot recently. They have a twelve-year-old son who is transitioning to become a girl. "We're just following our child's lead," they said.

Just following his lead.

Men, you don't follow the lead of a twelve-year-old. Those middle school years are some of the toughest years of our lives. We're fighting for who we are. We've got peer pressure. We're trying to figure out what to do with those crazy hormones raging through our bodies. Do you remember those years? Painful. Hard. "Who am I? Where do I fit?" The last thing these children need is to have the point man in their lives go AWOL.

Those years are when they need your strong and wise fatherly guidance.

That's when you love them.

That's when you lead them.

The father's mark on his boys and girls lasts a lifetime. That's because, whether you realize it or not, you're a compass. And by your life and your teaching, you are pointing them to the Lord Jesus Christ and His life-giving ancient boundaries.

8

HOW TO RAISE MASCULINE SONS AND FEMININE DAUGHTERS

*Men are generally more careful of the breed of their
horses and dogs than of their children.*

—William Penn

The compass has been around for two thousand years,
but it is still very valuable, even in our high-tech world.
I actually have one on my iPhone, and as I'm writing this
facing my computer screen, I am literally facing true north,
which reads 0 degrees N. True north is actually a little un-
comfortable, because I've got my chair turned slightly to the
right, and if I stay in this position for another ten minutes,
I'm going to have to visit my chiropractor. But when I turn
my chair slightly to my left, I'm no longer at 0 degrees
north—I'm at 344 degrees north.

I don't have to be facing true north to write this chapter. But if I were lost in the mountains, it would be incredibly helpful to be able to find true north and get my bearings.

Over the past thirty-five years, I've done a lot of research on raising masculine sons and feminine daughters. It hit me one day that Ephesians 6:4 was true north on this issue. Ephesians 6:4 gives the compass every Christian father needs to safely lead his children through the cultural confusion that increasingly surrounds us and causes so many to lose their way. Every piece of research I have regarding the development of a child's sexual identity is either directly or indirectly related to this one verse. Every book, every article, every quote, and every statistic merely reflects—from different perspectives—the principles contained in Ephesians 6:4:

> Fathers, do not provoke your children to anger, but bring them up in the discipline and *instruction of the Lord*.

According to *Merriam-Webster*'s dictionary, a compass is "a device for determining directions by means of a magnetic needle . . . turning freely on a pivot and pointing to the magnetic north."[1] A compass orients us in confusing circumstances and leads us toward our desired destination.

That describes exactly the role of a father. Just as a compass has four key marks—north, south, east, and west—so a Christian father is given four clear directions for pointing his children to their God-given identities.

An Ephesians 6:4 father is the compass his boys read to find the path to masculinity and his girls read to find the road to femininity.

But this passage goes far beyond sexual identity. Our

world wants to sum people up by their sexual orientation. It tells us that sex *is* our identity. But the Bible says that we are more than sexual beings. We are spiritual beings created in the image of God. It's what sets us apart from all other creatures.

When we father our children as spiritual beings, we lay a foundation that shapes them at their very core. We are pointing them to the Lord who created them. We are leading them to their deepest calling and purpose, *out of which sexual identity flows.*

That is why the wisdom of God is so superior to the wisdom of man. The instructions He gives to dads are timeless, no matter the world in which they are fathering. God's instructions were wise in the first century. And they are wise today. So that's where we will begin.

Let's jump into Ephesians 6:4 and pull out the timeless reference points God has given to fathers for raising their children. Once we've got our bearings, we'll apply this to the question of our children's sexual identities.

MORAL LANDMARK #1: FATHERS SHOULD RAISE THEIR CHILDREN IN FAIRNESS

If a man is fair with his kids, he will not provoke them to anger. A passage in Colossians parallels Ephesians 6:4:

> Fathers, do not exasperate your children, so that they will not lose heart. (3:21)

The idea behind the word *exasperate* is "do not embitter." This complements perfectly the word translated "provoke . . .

to anger" in Ephesians 6:4. The meaning is "to anger, to make angry, to bring one along to a deep-seated anger."[2]

All children complain that life isn't fair (which, of course, it isn't) and get angry when they don't get their way. Like us, our children are sinners by nature. We should expect them to push back against the godly fathering they so desperately need.

On the other hand, deep-seated anger in children springs from continual and habitual unfair treatment. It comes from father-wounds inflicted by controlling, domineering fathers or by passive fathers who won't step up to the plate for them.

Wouldn't that kind of treatment make you angry? Of course it would. You may know exactly what I'm talking about because that's how your father treated you. And that's why you've struggled with bitterness and resentment toward him for so many years. I'm sure you don't want to repeat that kind of behavior with your kids. It may not have fouled up your sexual identity, but unless I miss my guess, it sure has put a damper on your life.

Commentator William Hendriksen described it this way: "A child frequently irritated by over severity or injustice, to which, nevertheless, it must submit, acquires a spirit of sullen resignation, leading to despair."[3] What a terrible way to grow up! Hendriksen suggested there are at least six ways a father can embitter his children.[4]

1. *By overprotection.* It's natural to look at our world and fear for our children. But when we parent out of fear, we can become too high-control and pull the leash too tight. The result is a smothering home that engenders bitterness.

Overprotection may be the most effective way in the world to feminize a young boy. I have stacks of articles that substantiate this fact.

2. *By favoritism.* Isaac favored Esau over Jacob, and Rebekah preferred Jacob over Esau. And as we know, the trouble this brought on that family has reached down through the generations to this day. Favoritism creates an inflated or deflated self-perception, and saddest of all, the unfavored child loses sight of the fact that he is fearfully and wonderfully made. If you don't think favoritism can embitter a child, watch the classic movie *Ordinary People*. Enough said.

3. *By discouragement.* Habitual messages from fathers to children like "You'll never amount to anything" or "Can't you do anything right?" can plague children for the rest of their lives. This is one of the easiest ways to embitter children without realizing what you're doing. It can easily become a habit we are unaware of . . . a deadly habit.

4. *By forgetting that the child is growing up, has a right to have ideas of his own, and need not be an exact copy of his father.* I have often said to men that if you want a clone of yourself, put your face on the Xerox machine and run off a few copies. Let your kids be themselves.

5. *By neglect.* Child psychiatrist Robert Coles hit the nail on the head on this one:

> I think that what children in the United States desperately need is a moral purpose. They're getting parents who are very concerned about getting them into the right colleges, buying the best clothing for

them, giving them an opportunity to live in neighborhoods where they'll lead fine and affluent lives and where they can be given the best toys, go on interesting vacations, and all sorts of things. . . . Parents work very hard these days; and they're acquiring things that they feel are important for their children. And yet vastly more important things are not happening. *They're not spending time with their children*, at least not very much.[5]

6. *By bitter words and outright physical cruelty.* Most men who are verbally or physically abusive were treated that way as children. If that is your situation, I encourage you to break the chain. There are trained counselors who can help you. It will take some courage to admit your problem, but the generations to come will benefit from your willingness to admit your weakness.

MORAL LANDMARK #2: FATHERS SHOULD RAISE THEIR CHILDREN WITH TENDERNESS

The next command to fathers in Ephesians 6:4 is to "bring them up." The word translated as "bring them up" means "to nourish, to provide for with tender care."[6] Tenderness is a sensitivity toward others.

Masculine men are tender men. This does not mean they cease being strong with their children; it just means there is a tender side to their strength.

Children can quickly become embittered toward fathers when tenderness is missing.

Allow me to let you in on a secret: it's easier for me to define tenderness than to practice it. This is a weakness of mine. Some people are tender by personality and temperament. I am not. It's something I've spent a lifetime learning how to overcome, because if I allow it to go unchecked, I may end up embittering my children. And now I have grandchildren. I can't give myself permission to ignore this as I get older, and neither can you. That's why I work on it every day of my life. Unfortunately, as a father, I know I'm not alone in this weakness, so let's take a closer look at it.

Tenderness has different facets like a carefully cut diamond. If you look at tenderness from one angle, you'll see sympathy. From another, you'll notice compassion. Tenderness also carries the postures of responsiveness, warmth, and kindness.

Our children need to feel these things from us (from our wives too).

It is especially important that fathers be tender toward their daughters. A man who does not convey acceptance, warmth, tenderness, and compassion can easily embitter his daughter. If a young girl has a warm, loving, and tender relationship with her father, she will not bring into marriage the deeply embedded feelings of alienation that afflict young women without such dads. She will intuitively expect her husband to treat her in a tender way, just as her father treated her. She will look to marry a man with the same positive, tender characteristics she enjoyed with her father.

Let me suggest five tips that can help a man develop tenderness with his children:

1. *Listen to them and respect their feelings.* Children need to feel that you are the kind of father who

stops and listens. You want your kids to come to you about the concerns of their hearts rather than turning to their peers, who are as confused as they are.

2. *If you have been wrong or too harsh with them, be man enough to clearly confess and admit your wrongdoing and ask their forgiveness.* Don't make excuses; make a confession. As Corrie ten Boom is credited with saying, "The blood of Jesus never cleansed an excuse." Don't say, "I'm sorry if I was wrong"; say, "I was wrong. It was my fault." Spell it out with a repentant heart, and they will respect you and grow in their love for you.

Although it happened many years ago, I still remember blowing up at my then ten-year-old daughter, Rachel, just before bedtime. Actually, I blew up about forty-five minutes after she was supposed to be in bed. It had been a long day, and I was extremely tired. For some reason, she kept lingering and hovering around the house. I wanted peace and quiet. Finally, Mount Saint Helens blew. I'm sure the neighbors wondered what had so angered me. I told Rachel that she had fifteen seconds to be in bed—I repeated, *in* her bed.

She went to bed crying as the hot lava of my wrath pursued her up the stairs. After I came back down, Mary told me there were several good reasons she had been up. Some special event was to take place at school the next morning, and Rachel was getting ready for it. She wasn't lingering; she was preparing.

I felt like a real jerk. If I had bothered to ask Rachel what was going on, I could have discovered that for myself. But I didn't. I just vented on her. I made my way back up the stairs (careful not to step in the remaining pools of lava) and asked her forgiveness. We prayed together, and I tucked her in and decided the safest place for me was in bed as well. I told Mary I was turning in.

But I couldn't drop off to sleep. My explosion had unsettled me too. I kept thinking of the enormous damage I could inflict on my exquisite ten-year-old daughter without even realizing it. The last thing I wanted to do was crush her delicate spirit. Although we had patched it up and she had forgiven me, I couldn't get her off my mind.

After an hour or so, I got up, got in the car, and drove down to the twenty-four-hour supermarket. I found a red rose in a nice little vase and a card with a man peering out of a doghouse, and I headed home. I wrote Rachel a note telling her that I really did love her and that I really was wrong. Then I placed the rose and the card on the kitchen table. It was the first thing she saw the next morning when she walked into the kitchen.

I figured that after ruining her evening, the least I could do was make her day. It was worth the late-night trip. Instead of going off to school with memories of the red-hot lava, she could think of her serene red rose . . . and a dad who was genuinely sorry.

3. *Listen to the input your wife gives you about each child.* Usually, she is more in tune with their emotional needs than you are. She can be a tremendous resource—but you have to listen to her.

4. *Be "high touch" and dispense liberal doses of encouragement to both sons and daughters* (and don't forget your wife while you're at it). You can never be too encouraging. I don't say that lightly. Author John Trent calls this "the blessing." Give your kids verbal encouragement every time you turn around. It will nourish them and give them life.
5. *Consider their temperaments.* I have more to say about this later, but some children by their very temperaments require an extra dose of tenderness from their fathers. Stay tuned.

MORAL LANDMARK #3: FATHERS SHOULD RAISE THEIR CHILDREN WITH FIRMNESS

The third reference point of Ephesians 6:4 is that children are to be brought up "in the discipline and instruction of the Lord." The purpose of discipline and instruction is to build moral character into your children.

Discipline has to do with training. It comes from the idea of discipleship, which is your greatest privilege as a dad. No one can know your children and disciple them like you can. When you discipline, you're building your child's moral character.

Instruction is at the heart of training a child. When you teach, you are developing your children's understanding of God and His good plan for living life. If you don't teach them how to think and develop their worldviews, someone else will. You dare not leave this huge responsibility to schools or caregivers or, God forbid, peers. You must be sure your children are learning it from you. And don't instruct them in a mechanical, cold, and clinical way but rather in the warmth of a nurturing relationship.

The Firm Side of Love

Discipline and instruction are the firm side of love. To be firm is to be strong, steady, and resolute. When children push against the rules, they are saying, "Do you love me enough to hang tough with me? Am I worth the fight? Are you strong enough to handle me? Do you really care?" Firmness says, "Yes!" Every child, whether strong willed or compliant, needs his father's firm, directing hand.

The best primer in the world on how to teach and train your children is the book of Proverbs. It's an absolute treasure trove of advice for fathers who want to do this right.

Here are five guidelines as a summary:

1. A father who is firm takes the lead.
2. A father who is firm establishes boundaries.
3. A father who is firm lays out clear consequences.
4. A father who is firm is consistent.
5. A father who is firm is balanced.

Children need fathers who are willing to take charge.

Do you take the lead in matters of discipline in your home, or do you leave it to your wife? According to Ephesians 6:4, it is clearly *your* responsibility. That doesn't mean, of course, that your wife doesn't discipline the children. But it does mean you are the one who sets the standards, enforces the standards, models the standards, and appropriately disciplines when the standards are violated.

Although you take the lead in disciplining the children, make sure you and your wife are on the same page. If you disagree, ask the Lord to give you a oneness of mind.

Children need to know what the limitations are. They need fathers who love them enough to set reasonable rules and boundaries. And then they need their dads to establish clear consequences and rewards. Our children aren't capable of handling what the world says they can handle. They are innocent, naive, impressionable, and easily traumatized. Boundaries teach our children right and wrong and build a fence of protective security and love at the same time. Consequences train them to stay in those boundaries. Rewards encourage them in their growing character and maturity.

But consequences mean very little unless they are consistent. There is nothing more confusing and disheartening to children than ever-changing boundary lines or capricious consequences. Children crave consistency. Dad, you and I must be consistent—rain or shine, sleep deprived or rested, or at the end of our ropes. If you begin to realize that your consequences are too severe, have the wisdom to back off and explain why. If you realize that your consequences are not adequate, look for better ways to get through to your children. And again, be willing to explain yourself.

You may become aware of the need for certain boundaries and consequences only late in the game. But as long as your children are under your roof, it is never too late.

Finding Balance

The great challenge for every father is finding the balance between tenderness and firmness.

I remember when my dad taught me how to tie a Windsor knot in a necktie. I stood next to him with a tie in my hand.

He stood beside me with his. We were both facing the mirror as he walked me through the steps. We did it over and over until I finally got it.

Our heavenly Father wants to teach us how to tie another kind of knot and wrap it around our necks:

> Do not let kindness and truth leave you;
> Bind them around your neck. (Proverbs 3:3)

"Kindness and truth" is interchangeable with "tenderness and firmness." Fathers are to be firm at times and flexible and tender at other times. It takes the wisdom of God to know which is appropriate. The good news is that He will give us wisdom: "I will instruct you and teach you in the way which you should go; I will counsel you with My eye upon you" (Psalm 32:8).

Ephesians 6:4 instructs us to be ready to be firm or to be flexible at the appropriate time. But you, as the head, are always to lead your children. That is so important to God that a man who does not manage his own home well is not eligible for leadership in the church (see 1 Timothy 3:5).

Good fathers constantly try to achieve a balance between firmness and tenderness.

MORAL LANDMARK #4: FATHERS SHOULD RAISE THEIR CHILDREN "IN THE . . . LORD"

We've come full circle to where we began this chapter. God has commanded that in all we do, we are to raise our children "in the . . . Lord."

"A child is not a machine," Martyn Lloyd-Jones said.

"Christian parents must always remember that they are handling a life, a personality, a soul."[7]

It's our job, as the "high priests" of our families, to speak to our children's souls. To teach them where the values they are learning come from. To open their eyes to the nature of the God who created the world and put them in it. God has commanded Christian dads to instill in their children a love for and healthy fear of the Lord. "The fear of the LORD is the beginning of wisdom" (Proverbs 9:10). This fear is not about angst and anxiety. Rather, it's a healthy deep respect and awe. Just as they love and respect you, their earthly father, you want them to come to love and respect their heavenly Father.

Children who come to know the greatness and otherness of the living God will have hope in a despairing world. Children who learn to trust the sovereign, loving character of the Lord will have stability in the storms. Children who gain appreciation and respect for His Word will have a compass in the midst of complete confusion.

Who else is going to tell your children about Jesus Christ? You hope your church will do this. But that's not enough. *You* are the go-to guy on your family mission field. It's up to you to open your Bible in your home. It's up to you to draw attention to God's words at applicable moments. It's up to you to lead your family in prayer—to pray with your children when they are facing times of need. You are the point man who points them to Jesus.

In the right environment, at the right ages, children are astonishingly quick to learn. And what they have learned in their youth, they will never forget (see Proverbs 22:6).

In their excellent book *A Practical Guide to Culture*, John

Stonestreet and Brett Kunkle wrote about gender confusion and what fathers must do:

> Be a strong yet gentle father. Give your kids the three As—*attention, affection,* and *affirmation.* . . . Affirm your son's masculinity and mentor him into the world of men. For a more sensitive boy, connect with him and affirm his unique personality. With daughters, be affectionate from the beginning. Show respect and appreciation for their feminine distinctives.[8]

Deep within the four landmarks of Ephesians 6:4 are those very three *a*'s: attention, affection, and affirmation. Now it's time to apply them specifically to the development of your children's sexual identities. When we do this, we are giving them a huge head start in becoming comfortable in their God-given genders.[9]

A FOUNDING FATHER AND HIS SON'S SEXUALITY

When it comes to your son's sexual development, you must become a Founding Father. By that phrase I mean that you must help your son *find out* about how the Lord has hardwired him from the time he was created in the womb (see Psalm 139:13–16).

As a Founding Father, you should understand the stages of your son's development. Speaker and ministry leader Ricky Chelette laid out the natural stages of a boy's life for us.[10] Until the age of three, a little boy naturally *connects with both Mom and Dad.* It's important that he connects with both.

To the benefit of millennials, in recent years far more emphasis has been placed on a father's connection with his tiny infant. Dads used to stay at a distance until their boys could give them meaningful feedback. Now we know there's an explosion of learning going on in a little boy's brain in his earliest days. If he starts off being close to you, hearing your voice, and looking into your eyes, he knows you are safe and comfortable. When you roll around on the floor with him, bathe and dress him, hug and kiss him, and applaud his first steps and words, he learns that his primary role model is attentive, affectionate, and affirming. When you say no and mean it, he gains an early respect for you.

Two things need to happen for the healthy development of your son's male identity from ages four to ten:

1. A boy needs to *enjoy a special connection with his dad.* In this six-year span, a boy should be gradually disconnecting from his mom because he is instinctively identifying more with you. He's not rejecting her; she's still special and he still wants her nurture and care. But he should increasingly prefer to hang out with you.

2. A boy needs to *strongly connect with at least one other boy his age.* This means they can't wait to hang out and play together; they become best friends, go on family outings together, fight, explore, and hug each other at times of celebration.

Amazingly, by the end of these few in-between years, a young boy's gender is grounded. That's why you don't want to miss out on those years. Your focused presence and time with him are major parts of cementing his male identity. You're the Founding Father, but if you're gone all the time, you're not going to have the input in his life that he desperately needs. By age eleven, your son should basically have what Chelette called a "man-card."[11]

Personality and Masculine Development

Shakespeare was right when he wrote, "It is a wise father that knows his own child."[12] Founding Fathers must learn the personalities and temperaments of their sons. Just like their male DNA, their personalities were also hardwired by God before they came out of the womb. You want to discover that hardwiring and work with it, not try to change it.

Generally speaking, boys fall into three categories. Of course these aren't hard and fast; your son can fall anywhere across the spectrum. But for our purposes here, you'll begin to notice that your son lands somewhere within these three.

First, you've got the *rough and tumble;* second, you've got the *rough and tumble/sensitive,* and third, there's the *extremely sensitive.* These three categories can help you determine where your boy is on the spectrum. And once you figure that out, your job is to meet the needs that come with his hardwiring.

The majority of boys are more naturally rough and tumble. These guys are easy to spot: They tend to express their emotions physically. They tackle one another, punch holes through walls, and move through space at high speed. They enjoy doing things in groups of boys. They like to run outside and play with things that make noise or allow them to be active. Their typical choices in sports are football, basketball, baseball, soccer, and hockey. It isn't unusual to hear them use words like *whoosh* or *boom* when describing an incident.

These boys will tend to need more help putting words to their emotions. And they may have a harder time sitting still and staying focused in school. The best scholars agree that schools are designed around a girl's hardwiring. The teacher may not understand, but you can. And you can reassure your wife that her son's struggle is as normal as the sun rising in the sky. Also, many of these boys' skill sets don't fall into the areas that get attention in a classroom. This is why so many boys today don't feel gifted and smart. But you can reassure your sons that they are gifted and smart—every son is. They need to know there are many other kinds of "smart" besides the kind measured on a school test.

Sometimes a boy's skill is being people savvy, having the ability to read and influence people, which is a great gift. Sometimes it's a mechanical or artistic ability that can't be taught; it's just there from birth. Sometimes it's a vigorous imagination. You can take note of your son's gifts and remind him that his gifts will shine in due time.

Should he do his best in school? Absolutely. But he does it with perspective. There's nothing more magnificent to a boy than a father who "gets" him and believes in him.

The second group of boys has a higher level of sensitivity mixed in with their rough-and-tumble nature. They like to be active, but they also like to work quietly for hours at a time—building Legos, reading books, doing other projects with their hands like cutting, drawing, and designing. They enjoy being with a group of boys, but they're comfortable being buddies with girls or just playing alone.

When it comes to sports, they can enjoy group sports or

solo sports. But at the end of the day, they would choose hanging out with their dad over their mom, and they get plenty of physical interaction with other boys.

These boys need a dad who will enjoy their rough-and-tumble activity but also engage with them one on one. They may talk readily with their mom, but they also need you to talk with them about what they are feeling. They need a man's perspective and input.

The third group of boys is much smaller—3 to 5 percent of boys. They are extremely sensitive, and their parents may not even realize it because their sensitivity is a prominent feature of their interior lives. These boys walk around with a big magnifying glass attached to the lens of their souls. On the outside they may appear to be somewhat typical, but in their minds, they are experiencing everything that happens to them or around them *much* more significantly and intensely. They take it all in and feel it deeply. These boys are wired to primarily express themselves in more creative ways: writing, drama, music, drawing, and so on. They are also more verbal in expressing their emotions than other boys. They won't gravitate as much to groups of boys, and they are often drawn to solo-oriented sports.

Here's what you need to know: these sensitive young men are not gay. However, the culture, and others around them, will tell them that they are gay. But a father's involvement in their lives will negate these satanic lies. They are male through and through and are incredibly gifted. God has given them this hardwiring for a purpose. Oftentimes they are dreamers and visionaries. Many go on to radically affect the world. But it's important for you to know that in the area of sexuality, these boys end up being most at risk for moving toward homosexuality—especially in today's world. This is because they don't feel they fit into the male pack and don't tend to get the normal male touch and interplay with their rough-and-tumble peers. They feel different from most boys. If their dads aren't around to affirm them, *masculinity becomes a mystery.*

That's why your relationship with this son early in life is so important. Dads need to be especially careful to give this son one-on-one attention. Nine times out of ten, you're not as highly sensitive as he is. You may even feel you're speaking a different language than he speaks. But don't let that throw you. Both of you are guys. You can still draw close to him and track with him.

Highly sensitive boys need a lot more eyeball-to-eyeball contact with their dad. And don't forget, these boys are more verbal. While other boys are content to be in *proximity* with Dad, repairing a car, throwing a ball, or doing a building project, highly sensitive boys have a greater need for your focused *presence.* This means getting down on their level and looking them in the eyes, talking openly with them, and drawing close to them one on one.

If your sensitive son won't look you in the eyes, chances are he doesn't feel secure revealing himself to you. That's when you need to pray that the Lord will break down the barrier. That's also when you work extra hard at finding a way to reach him. To him, you are larger than life.

A sensitive boy tends to be a people pleaser, and he's especially sensitive to your approval. He's terrified that you would disapprove if you could see inside his soul. He doesn't want to displease you or rock the boat. Here's where you must become intentional: take him on one-on-one outings of his choice; make a special point of letting down your hair and sharing your own struggles and fears from your growing-up years; ask him questions about his thoughts and dreams and fears. He will begin to feel he has an inside track to your heart, and vice versa. The intimidation factor will fall away, and he will begin to feel close to you.

Many fathers have preconceived ideas of how their sons should act and what they should be interested in. *But let me say this again: God made your son in His image, not yours.*

Let's say you like hunting. He loves reading and, to be honest, isn't a fan of hunting. Your disappointment feels like rejection to him. This is when you decide to learn something about reading. You go get a book that he loves and you read it with him. You start a father-son reading relationship. The talking that would have happened while hunting (when you weren't sitting stone quiet in a deer blind) now happens as you are discussing a book. Maybe one day he will decide to join you on a hunting trip, but if not, it's no big deal. You're stepping outside your box and confirming that God intends to use this boy to influence the world in ways you never will.

A highly sensitive boy who doesn't have that kind of warm, accepting relationship with his dad will identify more with his mom. In the absence of strong men (especially if he is surrounded by women, like grandmothers, aunts, and sisters), he will identify even more with the feminine model. He'll gravitate primarily toward friendships with girls. Why? Because rough-and-tumble boys can be very hard on a sensitive boy; they can gang up on him and bully him. Girls are more verbal; girls aren't as rough in their play; girls are safer. The female world will become his comfort zone. Eventually, girls will become his object of sexual identity rather than his object of sexual attraction.

You don't want that to happen. You want your son to be extremely comfortable around men.

When I was a kid, in the summers after an early dinner, our family would go swimming at a new aquatic center near our home. Afterward, my brothers and I would follow my dad into the shower to get the chlorine off us. That was a lesson for the three of us. When we were eight, six, and four, we learned some lessons about our future masculinity just by soaping up and rinsing off. That's all part of learning about gender from Dad. It was no big deal; it was just a natural part of life.

A sensitive son shouldn't be pampered when he gets hurt any more than any other boy. If you are calm, he'll be calm. Don't push him, but draw him into esteem-building activities he might not normally tackle as a young man, like hiking or climbing or taking a karate class. Teach him how to stand up for himself and fend off the bullies. Encourage him to venture into friendships with other boys. He needs only one or two friends to put him on his way.

The more you do these kinds of things, the more you will build his self-esteem and solve the mystery of masculinity in his life. And the more you will help him become comfortable in his own gender.

The Pivotal Stage

From ages eleven to sixteen, puberty hits. It's the crazy period when a boy's hormones increase 600 percent, carrying him all over the map and creating all kinds of new feelings and identity issues. (You've been through it, so you know what I mean.)

It's too big a subject to cover here. I would say just two things: First, the best resource on this subject is the book *Preparing for Adolescence*, by Dr. James Dobson. Second, you have to watch your son's friends during these years. Friends are *huge*. Wild boys can appear to be perfectly nice guys inside your home, but "do not be deceived: Bad company ruins good morals" (1 Corinthians 15:33, ESV). You need to have your ear very close to the ground when it comes to the company your son is keeping. Don't ignore red flags. As a Founding Father, you hold veto power over your son's friends.

When classes on sexuality at school lay out the option that he could be gay (and in a public school, you can be sure this is happening), his hidden feelings may take on a sense of urgency. It's not unusual that by the time this at-risk son is fifteen, he will be searching on the internet for someone who understands. Too often he will find that person in a man twice his age who will say, "I totally identify; I've gone through the same thing. You were born gay, like me." Your son will begin to interpret himself based on the lens of someone older, someone misguided, someone helping to set a course he doesn't feel he can avoid.

You head this off early in his life by interacting closely with him. And when you do that, he will feel understood. He will have no need to find a man who understands him, because his dad already does.

And by all means, *watch out for predators.*

Many homosexual men were abused by men when they were young. If your son is in a sport, guard over his coaches like a hawk and talk with him about what constitutes inappropriate touch. Tell him to let you know if anyone ever tries to touch him inappropriately.

Every young man—no matter his personality—needs a Founding Father. Every son needs a father who believes in him. Every son needs to feel close to his dad and be able to talk with him about anything. Every son needs a dad who sees his gifts and takes the time to help him set the direction for his life.

When you give your son this kind of attention, warm affection, and—most important—your stamp of approval, you are solidifying his masculine identity.

WHEN CHILDREN WALK AWAY

Over the years, I have had many fathers share their broken hearts with me. They have raised boys who have become practicing homosexuals, and the guilt these dads feel is unbearable. They are looking for where they went wrong and what they could have done differently.

If I were talking with them today, I would tell them about Christopher Yuan.

Christopher was a brilliant, sensitive, often-bullied young boy. In his teen years he became addicted to pornography and eventually moved into the gay lifestyle. While he was studying in dental school, he began selling drugs and making money hand over fist. A few months before he was to graduate, he failed miserably in his grades and was put out of school. His mother, who had become a believer, began praying: "Lord, do whatever it takes to save him." A few weeks later, twelve federal agents burst into his home and caught him red-handed with drugs. It was over.

While in prison he just "happened" to see a Gideon Bible

in the trash can. Out of sheer boredom he began reading it. He looked at every passage in Scripture that dealt with homosexuality and came to the realization, "It's sin. It's always sin. I'm a sinner."

Then he was transferred to a prison in Kentucky. He had lost all hope because he was going to be there for seventy-two months. He had ruined his life. When he walked into his new cell and flopped onto the bottom bunk, it was his lowest time ever. Looking up at the plywood beneath the top mattress, these words had been scribbled: "If you're bored, read Jeremiah 29:11." He grabbed his Bible and read, " 'For I know the plans that I have for you,' declares the LORD, 'plans for welfare and not for calamity to give you a future and a hope.' " That's when Christopher gave his life to Christ.

That was many years and another life ago. Today, Yuan is a professor at Moody Bible Institute and ministers all over the country to those who are struggling. In one of his books, *Holy Sexuality and the Gospel,* Yuan wrote, "Certainly parents can have positive and negative influences on their children, but *influence is not the same as cause.*"[13] His parents were not the cause of his homosexuality. The root cause for his choice in life was sin. His problem was the problem in every one of us: we are all sinners who are born apart from God and in need of forgiveness and redemption.

If you have a child who has walked away—whether he has renounced his faith or gotten into addiction or fallen into a lifestyle of any sin, including homosexuality—here is what Christopher Yuan would say to you: God does not want you to carry around the guilt of your children's choices. Your children make their own choices. And some children walk away. Perhaps you did that at some point in your own life. There is no ironclad promise that your child will always walk in the truth.

The second chapter of this book is titled "Save the Boys." The upcoming chapter is titled "Save the Girls." But what do I mean by "save"? It's to "intentionally move toward and influence" them. I'm not talking about eternal salvation. Only the Lord can do that. He did it for you and me. He has to do it for each of our children.

We don't determine the influences and course of events in the lives of our children. We don't determine how they will respond. And we certainly don't determine how they will enter the kingdom. Jesus alone, by the work of the Holy Spirit, draws hearts and minds. Jesus alone saves them and keeps them. This is why our Lord told the parable of the prodigal son (see Luke 15:11–32). Sometimes children have to come to the end of themselves before the Lord grabs hold of their hearts. God knows what He's about. God has His ways and His times.

Christopher Yuan, like so many others who have been saved out of the homosexual lifestyle—people like Rosaria Butterfield and Becket Cook—brought nothing to Christ but broken lives and repentant hearts. And they are living proof that there is always hope for grieving fathers.

God asks only two things of fathers: First, He asks us to be pliable and willing to learn, no matter our age or the mistakes we have made. Second, He asks us to trust Him to do His work as we are praying diligently. As one wise pastor prayed,

We know it is thy power alone that can recall wandering children,

and can impress on them a sense of divine things,
and can render that sense lasting and effectual.[14]

In other words, the Lord knows how to penetrate a hard heart and do the necessary surgery that leads to regeneration and eternal life.

So keep praying—and keep trusting the greatest Founding Father of all.

SAVE THE GIRLS

If our daughters are to flower, they too need optimal growing conditions.

—Evelyn Bassoff

In Joshua 14:6–14, Caleb is described as a man who "followed the Lord . . . fully" (verse 8). Or to put it another way, he followed the Lord with his whole heart. At the age of forty, this man of great faith, along with Joshua, was willing to take on the giants in the Promised Land that turned ten other leaders into contemptible cowards. It's a famous history lesson recorded for us in Numbers 13 and 14.

Not only was Caleb a man of great faith, but he was also a great father to his daughter, Achsah, as we read in Joshua 15:18–19:

She alighted from the donkey, and Caleb said to her, "What do you want?" Then she said, "Give me a blessing; since you have given me the land of the Negev, give me also springs of water." So he gave her the upper springs and the lower springs.

All the land in that area of the Negev was desert, and rainfall was nearly nonexistent. Achsah, who had just been married, undoubtedly hoped for children in the future. Those children would need to be fed and nourished. If her father would give her the springs, her family could grow crops, and the land would be a great asset for generations.

It's no stretch to say that by granting her request and giving her the upper springs and the lower springs, Caleb saved his daughter. People without water can die in a desert, but never-ending springs of water provide a way to survive.

You may not have any springs in your backyard to give your daughter. That's not a problem, because you have other gifts to provide, gifts she desperately needs for her future survival and well-being.

In this book, we've spent a lot of time talking about raising sons because they will be the spiritual leaders of their families in the next generation. In the original *Point Man,* the second chapter was also "Save the Boys," and that's still a critical topic. But in the original book, I didn't have a chapter titled "Save the Girls." Well, here it is.

If you don't have a daughter, you should probably still read this chapter. Are you married? Well, your wife is a daughter. Is it possible there were some things she needed from her father that he did not provide? You can become a better husband right now by getting to know her needs so that you can live with her in an understanding way.

God wired men and women to be different. I remember when my wife brought two pieces of painted wood into a house we were building. She plopped them in the light against the wall and said, "I think the second color is the best." The builder and I couldn't tell the difference. "Yep," said the builder. "Women see more shades of color than men do." I didn't believe it until I googled it.

Men and women are different not only in their body physiology but also in the wiring of their brains, in their hormones, and in their emotional makeup. All of this was intended by the Creator. He made a woman in His image— equal to the man, yet different. He made her to fit the man, to respond to him, and to complement him. I, for one, am very glad.

I need the women God has given to me, and you need the women God has given to you. They bring strengths and perspectives we lack. They meet needs in our lives a guy can never meet. The challenge comes in understanding them. Since women are made by the Lord to be different from men, their development is a mystery to us. This may be the greatest challenge for any dad raising daughters: we've never been a girl.

I had two brothers but no sisters, so I probably had more to learn than most guys when it came to girls, women, wives, and daughters. Over the years, I've learned some things that have been very valuable—some through books and godly counselors, and some through making a lot of mistakes. Fortunately, the women in my life have been very patient with me.

In this chapter, I want to condense some of the truths I've learned along the way, facts that are extremely important for fathers to know about their daughters, as well as crucial realities about the times in which we're raising them. There are some very real threats to your daughter's well-being that you have to know about. But there are also just some basic facts about how the Lord has made and wired her that we dads can easily miss.

So let me give you some fast facts about females, specifically your daughter. Actually, I'm going to give you seven fast facts and two slow ones.

FAST FACT #1: GIRLS NEED RELATIONAL CONNECTION

The bottom line for your daughter is that she wants intimacy and connection. It drives everything in her life, including her sexuality. Guys are more visually driven in their sexuality. Girls are more relationally driven.

Did you get that? If you don't get anything else we say about girls, remember this: *intimacy and connection are the driving forces of your daughter's life.*

I don't care if your daughter is an aggressive, athletic tomboy. I don't care if she is less expressive or communicative than other girls. Your daughter has a deep need for intimacy and connection. It's a hallmark of the female sex.

You should also know that in this age of gender confusion, when those deep relational needs aren't met, you have a fertile soil for lesbianism. *Lesbianism is all about connection and intimacy gone awry.* We'll come back to that.

The bottom line for you as a dad is to find ways to be close to your daughter and connect with her heart. It may take a little work, but you can do that. She isn't looking to be cast in your image, but she does take her cues from you.

Dr. Meg Meeker, who has counseled hundreds of troubled girls, put it this way:

> [Your daughters] watch you intensely. They hang on your words. They hope for your attention, and they wait for it in frustration—or in despair. They need a gesture of approval, a nod of encouragement, or even simple eye contact. . . .
>
> When she's in your company, your daughter tries harder to excel. . . . Boyfriends, brothers, even husbands can't shape her character the way you do. You will influence her entire life because she gives you an authority she gives no other man.[1]

Your daughter doesn't need you to bottom-line and "fix" her problems; she just needs you to listen and understand. She needs you to look her in the eyes and connect.

That pretty much sums it up.

FAST FACT #2: GIRLS LONG TO FEEL SAFE

Girls feel affirmed when their dads *provide* for them. A dad who responsibly provides for his family financially helps his daughter experience the safety of being cared for. And fathers who step protectively between their daughters and the world make their daughters feel safe. Girls whose dads don't step up to protect them or provide for them tend to feel vulnerable and unloved. And that can create a "father wound." Father wounds can lead to a hard-edged exterior of independence hiding a deep inner hurt. In some cases, it can lead to a detachment from men altogether.

You want to be the kind of man you would want your daughter to marry one day—a godly, teachable man who is ready to care for her and lead her. She's going to weigh every guy who comes along against you. If you're a man of your word, she will look for a man who keeps his word. If you make her feel treasured, protected, and cared for, she's likely to choose a man who will do the same. And that's what you want for her, right?

When it comes to gender confusion, counselor and speaker D'Ann Davis explained how a father helps his daughter:

> A father possesses the ability to speak truth into chaos and affirm his daughter's female identity. She needs to hear, "You're special to me. You're beautiful. I love your heart. I delight in you. I will protect you. I will care for you. I'm proud of you. You have what it takes to be a strong and feminine woman." A father is strategic in helping his daughter get her "woman-card" before she even enters high school.[2]

Let me encourage you. Your daughter needs the same three *a*'s as your son: *attention, affection,* and *affirmation.* And I find that very reassuring and helpful.

FAST FACT #3: GIRLS PROCESS THEIR WORLD DIFFERENTLY THAN BOYS DO

Daughters can be a *mystery* for a dad. Boys are easier for a father to understand. They are more straightforward in their development than girls. Girls are more developmentally complex. They hit puberty earlier than boys. Their relationships with one another are more difficult to unscramble. Their sexual development is more nuanced.

Let's break that down. Girls have more layers; they are usually more verbal, deeply emotional, and continually in touch with what lies beneath the surface.

It's like they have a sixth sense. They can read us like a book, which can be eerily nerve-racking. And they are not as predictable to us. Men tend to read the lines, while women tend to read between the lines. That's because they are responding to a hundred different cues and processing them all on different levels.

Sometimes this can be as confusing to them as it is to you. In the midst of their confusion, they need your listening ear. They want you to *process* with them. That sounds like fun, doesn't it? Seriously, they want to know you're willing to walk with them through the labyrinth of their inner struggles and promise to be there on the other side.

Girls can also melt a father's heart, and they are very aware of that! My dad raised three boys. We could never get away with anything with him. But then along came the first two granddaughters. I have never seen my own dad turn into such a complete pile of putty as he did with those adorable girls.

But don't let your sweet little women talk you into letting them do things they are not ready for, things you intuitively know they cannot handle, situations that are not wise for them. It's good for them to hear no at times like that. It underscores that you are older and wiser and have their best interests in mind.

FAST FACT #4: GIRLS FACE SIGNIFICANT CHALLENGES AS THEY ENTER THEIR TEENS

When puberty hits, a girl's security is put to the test. Her body changes more obviously than boys' bodies, and some girls develop more quickly than others. Peer pressure intensifies. This is when they need your affirmation and approval more than ever.

In case you haven't noticed, girls are also different from boys in how they relate to one another. They hug a lot. They get excited and squeal. When they fight, they go after one another verbally, so their fights are not usually resolved in fisticuffs. Boys get angry, fight like dogs, and then walk away and call it a day. But—this may surprise you—girls can actually be meaner to one another than boys are, stabbing one another in the back and hurling deep, hurtful words that don't go away easily.

In adolescence, your daughter will struggle to feel accepted into the "woman club." She has to wear the right clothes, say the right things, and possess a mysterious magnet that will make her popular. Girls form cliques that can be terribly cruel.

It's important for your daughter to connect with her mom during these years. She needs to unload with a woman she looks up to so she is able to think clearly about what is happening around her. It also makes a difference if she can find a girlfriend who shares her convictions and wants to follow the Lord—someone she can open up with, talk to about boys, and safely bare her soul to. This is where church groups and girls' Bible studies can really make a difference.

Girls tend to be more spiritually aware than boys their age. And that's a good thing. They'll want to talk with you and your wife about their spiritual questions. That's also a good thing. Be glad when your daughter feels safe enough to go to you with any spiritual questions and struggles.

FAST FACT #5: GIRLS NEED HEALTHY BOUNDARIES

She will need your *direction*. Don't be reluctant to shepherd your daughter when it comes to dealing with less-than-honorable young men or bad friends and situations. It's your job to protect her and step in when the Lord prompts you by triggering your internal radar.

Since girls develop physiologically earlier than boys, it's easy for a dad to become lax and overestimate his daughter's maturity. In other words, she's still young and she doesn't have it all together. She needs you—your discernment and your leadership.

At your weakest moment, she will say, "Don't you trust me?" (All teenagers use this argument to manipulate their parents.) But you have to tell her that the wise boundaries you have in place *have nothing to do with trust and everything to do with keeping her safe and moving her in the right direction.*

Sadly, we live in a dangerous world. At least one in four girls is sexually molested before reaching adulthood.[3] Some of those acts are perpetrated by extended family or fathers of her friends. They can also come from church staff or male caregivers. So be on the alert.

You may be the only father you know who gives your daughter wise boundaries, but you can't let that stop you. You should resist letting her stay overnight with a girlfriend whose father you don't know and therefore cannot trust.

(It's better for girls to stay at your house anyway, where there is a father you do know . . . *you*.) And be alert when something doesn't seem right. You never know when a predator will show up. You and your wife have to talk with your daughter about inappropriate touch. You must do more than take her seriously if she says she has been abused. Dads must expose abuse when it happens and take steps to help their daughters get help for recovery.

You must provide a powerful defense against the enemy's attempts to destroy your little girl's healthy sexuality. You and your wife need to decide the appropriate age for both group and one-on-one dating. And don't give in to what other parents are allowing. Parents can be utterly foolish in this area; you don't need to be one of them. You can be strict and kind at the same time.

You'll definitely want to meet and size up every boy who comes to the door to pick her up. Be natural about it . . . but be there. Fathers tend to be able to sniff out the rotten apples.

I made it a point to be present when a young man first picked up my beautiful daughter. My goal was to instill just a little bit of fear in him without embarrassing her. You think I'm kidding, but I'm not. I would meet him at the door, look him in the eye, and—calling him by name (in a friendly way)—ask a few pertinent questions, like "Can you tell me about yourself?," "Where are you going?," and "You plan to be back by curfew, right?" I wanted him to know in a matter-of-fact way, one man to another, that he was handling a "Stradivarius" that needed to be returned in the same condition. The boy got the message.

It's important for you or your wife to be up when your daughter gets home. (That's true as well when your son is out on a date or at a social activity.) It's an accountability thing. What's the point in a curfew if no one ensures it is kept? (If you're exhausted, sleep on the couch while you wait.)

When you hug her as she comes in, watch her body language. Is she glad to see you? She should be. Your daughter may roll her eyes and even express resentment for your oversight, but deep down she knows you love her very much, and someday she'll thank you. Just hang in there, Dad. Chances are, many a bad choice or problematic relationship will be averted because of your intentional involvement in her life.

Virginity is mocked today. But a lovely young woman who commits to virginity has a special power. You can tell her about this. When she says no, she may also be keeping a testosterone-driven young man from losing his virginity. And she'll command his respect. You can tell her the male perspective: a *good man* will have immense respect for a woman who doesn't give away what should be given to only her husband.

"We have a popular culture that's not healthy for girls and young women," Meg Meeker said, "and there is only one thing that stands between it and your daughter. You."[4] A good dad may need to show up at a party where his daughter's friends (and maybe his daughter) have been drinking and take her home. Heart-to-heart conversations have to take place about how she got to the party in the first place and why a change in friends needs to happen.

You also might need to talk to her about the clothes she is about to wear out the door; you love her too much to let her cheapen herself through immodesty. She's too valuable to demean herself by exposing or flaunting her body.

Don't worry if your daughter becomes upset and there's a power struggle. You know this by now, but I'll say it once again: *she's giving you a test*. Calmly let her know that you love her too much to make tragic mistakes. She may say you're unfair. Be calm and don't surrender your leadership. She really wants to know, "Do you love me enough? Are you strong enough to handle me?" Your answer has to be yes.

Let me be clear. I'm not talking about being unnecessarily strict or socially weird or overbearing. There's a difference between being controlling and being wisely and appropriately protective. In today's world, dads have to find that balance. How might you accomplish this? Read on.

FAST FACT #6: GIRLS NEED DAD'S ACTIVE ENGAGEMENT

Your daughter needs your time, and she needs to talk. It's important for you to hang out with her, and if you notice little things about her, compliment her. Take her on dates or father-daughter trips. Write her notes of encouragement to let her know she's special. She will decide that if her dad likes her, maybe she's okay. Maybe she's going to make it through after all. Sometimes all she really wants is for her dad to just hold her and let her cry. Nothing is more reassuring than when a strong dad notices that his daughter is sad and pursues her and draws her out. Statistics show that girls "who spend more time with their fathers are less likely to drink, take drugs, have sex as teenagers, or have out-of-wedlock babies."[5]

Don't let your daughter fade into isolation when she shows signs of anxiety or depression. If she's not talking, something is going on. You and your wife have to care enough to find out what.

Fathers learn early on that girls tend to talk much more about their feelings than boys do. The women in my life never leave me wondering how they're feeling, even if it's through their uncharacteristic silence. That's just my experience. Not every girl fits this pattern, but most do. You can spend three hours watching a football game with your son and never say a word—and both of you would be happy. But most daughters aren't wired like that.

I've been told that a good rule of thumb is to use twice as many words with your daughter as you would in other conversations. A dad who talks with his daughter—eyeball to eyeball, one on one—is connecting with her. Your encouraging words can carry her through weeks or even months.

Mostly you just need to listen. So as exhausted and out of words as you are at the end of the day, try to find a way to summon up extra words for your daughter.

Are you separated for long periods from your daughter due to a divorce? Don't let that stop you from working hard to be close to her. You matter more to her than you can imagine.

In the book of Esther, we have a great example of a man named Mordecai who was forcibly separated from his adopted daughter, Esther, in an evil and dangerous time. But he did not let that stop him. He knew she needed his continued watchfulness and protection. So he went to the gates of the palace where she had been taken and found ways to communicate with her (see Esther 2:11, 19, 21). He prayed for her constantly and stayed closely involved with her. Time and again, God honored Mordecai's persistence. In the end, his watchful care over Esther saved her life.

By the grace of God, you, too, can be a Mordecai in your daughter's life. Rest assured, the Lord is for you—and for any dad who commits to faithfully carrying out his role despite tough predicaments. Just as He did for Mordecai, God will move to help you in the most unexpected ways.

FAST FACT #7: GIRLS NEED TO BE ASSURED OF THEIR INNATE BEAUTY

Your daughter will be pressured to starve herself to get the perfect body. In this image-obsessed culture, you shouldn't be surprised to learn that eating disorders are rampant among young women. When your pimply, blossoming daughter hits her adolescent years, she can't help but compare herself to the incessant images of sexy, beautiful women that bombard her day after day.

A girl who feels unloved and unlovely can begin to think the path to love and approval is through the perfect body, so she will stop eating. Her aim will be to get to a size 0. In case you don't know what that is, it's as skinny as it gets! Then she will imagine she has achieved physical perfection. But every time she steps on a scale or looks in the mirror, she won't see perfection.

Pay very close attention if your daughter begins to look unnaturally thin. This is how a girl becomes trapped in the vicious cycle of anorexia or bulimia.

From the time your daughter is very young, you can counter any thoughts that she isn't beautiful enough. Don't make the huge mistake of critiquing her body; that will devastate her and cause her to obsess even more.

"Charm is deceitful and beauty is vain," says the writer of Proverbs, "but a woman who fears the LORD, she shall be praised" (31:30). You can teach her this great truth. Praise your daughter's unique beauty and character—her eyes, her smile, her sense of humor, her quick intelligence, her strong work ethic, her tenderness or spunky passion, her wonderful way with people, or her spiritual discernment. Your praise is powerful. It negates the cesspool of daily messages that inundate her life. You're affirming that what matters is not a vain and shallow beauty but rather the inner beauty that shines from her heart, personality, and character.

Every girl wants to be beautiful to someone. You can be that someone.

Those are the seven fast facts.

Now it's time for the two slow facts. What I mean by slow is that you need to take your foot off the accelerator and tap the brakes, because there are a few dangerous curves ahead for your daughter, and if you don't navigate them carefully, the result may be tremendous damage.

You may want to grab a cup of coffee and reset your brain before you dive in. I say this because it will be easy for your mind to wander right about now, and you can't afford to let that happen. Satan doesn't want you to know what we are about to discuss. But you must know.

SLOW FACT #1: BIBLICAL FEMININITY IS UNDER ATTACK

The first curve is the influence of modern feminism, a spiritual cancer that has spread into every organ and cell of the modern body politic.

From early childhood, your daughter is told lies about her identity. You and your wife need to be aware of just how vulnerable she is to the messages of feminist ideology that lead her away from the design of God and ultimately kill her true femininity. Modern-day feminism hasn't thrown just biblical manhood under the bus; it has canceled biblical womanhood too. In its attack on the home, feminism directly targets our daughters. Over the years, feminism has grown into a cult religion, taking captive not only our culture but the church as well.

Ultimately, Satan is the father of feminism. In John 8:44, Jesus said that Satan is "the father of lies." Just as he deceived the man and woman in Genesis 3:4 ("You surely will not die!"), he deceives today. What are some of the lies our daughters are being told?

1. Feminism declares Christianity is the great enemy of women.
2. Feminism believes that "traditional" roles repress and stereotype women. Unfortunately, under the pretense of getting rid of stereotypes, feminism has eradicated feminine identity.
3. Feminism teaches that men are a threat to the ascendancy of women to their rightful place of authority.
4. Feminism claims that men and women are basically the same biologically, a position that is scientifically untenable. But in keeping with this lie, feminism goes on to assert that there are no real purposeful differences between the sexes. A woman can do anything a man can do, and roles can easily be reversed or interchanged.
5. Feminism stokes the fear that a woman is likely to lose her identity if she makes her family her top priority. She should look out for herself and focus on career success no matter what it costs her family.

6. Feminism discourages women from tending to the needs of their children, declaring, "Your children will be happy if you are happy." This is the same lie used to justify affairs and divorce, right?

7. Feminism insists a woman can have it all: successful career, great marriage, and happy, well-adjusted children. This is one of its most appealing lies.

8. Feminism cautions women against showing signs of feminine softness. If they want to be respected and get ahead, they should toughen up and become more like men.

9. Feminism says that a woman does not need a man for anything. Instead, she should strive for self-sufficiency and total independence.

The best way to counter any lie is with the truth. Jesus said, "If you continue in My word, then you are truly disciples of Mine; and you will know the truth, and the truth will make you free" (John 8:31–32).

You want your daughter to know the truth. You want her to be set free. So let's walk through some of the great truths that refute these deadly lies.

First, a woman's greatest friends are Jesus Christ and His teachings in Scripture. There has never been a greater advocate for women than Jesus, and historically, wherever the gospel has taken root around the globe, conditions for women have improved significantly. That's because the Bible teaches that women are created *different yet equal*. As believers, they are fellow heirs in the kingdom of God (see 1 Peter 3:7). They are to be cherished and loved sacrificially by their husbands (see Ephesians 5:25–30). And they are to be treated with equal honor, dignity, and value (see Galatians 3:28).

Second, godly manhood is a gift to women. This is the clear message of the book of Ruth. When Christian marriage is lived out as God commanded, husbands love their wives sacrificially, to the extreme. How extreme? "Just as Christ also loved the church and gave Himself up for her," said Paul in Ephesians 5:25. That's extreme. A woman who lives with this kind of man cannot help but flourish and thrive. Boaz did that for Ruth (see Ruth 4), and you can oppose the cult of feminism by leading with love in your home. There's nothing like a truly good and godly man to dispute the lies spewed by angry feminist doctrine.

Third, science tells us that men and women are different—physiologically, hormonally, psychologically, and even neurologically (in how our brains are wired). But the Bible explains why: God built differences into men and women to equip them to complement—not compete with—one another (see Genesis 2:18). He equipped men and women uniquely to fulfill their God-given roles. From creation, God wired into a woman's very DNA certain feminine traits suited for nurturing a home and children. This is a wonderful gift.

Can a man be nurturing? Sure, up to a point. Can a woman protect and provide for her family? Yes, and many moms do. But if we are honest about how life works best, our great Architect knew what He was doing when He created the differences between us. Someone has to protect and provide, and someone has to care for the home and the children.

"The family is the heart of society," said the great Harvard sociologist Pitirim A. Sorokin.[6] The family is not just an arm or a finger. It is the very heart. And when you have a bad heart, you're in serious trouble. Dr. Michael Novak put it this way: "One unforgettable law has been learned painfully through all the oppressions, disasters, and injustices of the last thousand years: *if things go well with the family, life is worth living; when the family falters, life falls apart.*"[7] There's no greater calling than that of sacrificially pouring into the lives of our children.

G. K. Chesterton wrote of the value of a mother's time with her children in their early years:

> [A mother of young children is] with a human being at the time when he asks all the questions that there are, and some that there aren't. . . . How can it be a large career to tell other people's children about the Rule of Three, and a small career to tell one's own children about the universe? . . . A woman's function is laborious, but because it is gigantic, not because it is minute.[8]

There is no more important work than motherhood, especially in this high-risk, upside-down world. Young children desperately need a mom who is willing to sacrificially focus her time and energy in their upbringing. And the Bible honors a woman's willingness to build her home and raise up her children:

> An excellent wife, who can find?
> For her worth is far above jewels. . . .
>
> She opens her mouth in wisdom,
> And the teaching of kindness is on her tongue.

She looks well to the ways of her household,
And does not eat the bread of idleness.
Her children rise up and bless her;
Her husband also, and he praises her, saying:
"Many daughters have done nobly,
But you excel them all." (Proverbs 31:10, 26–29)

Don't let the world "masculinize" your daughter. Encourage her to develop her gifts and move confidently into the world around her. As she does, *encourage her to be strong in her femininity.* It is one of her greatest assets, and it will take her to where the Lord wants her to go.

Oh, and by the way, *no one can have it all.* The best things in life always involve self-sacrifice. Everyone must make wise (and sometimes difficult) choices throughout the seasons of life. Mothering doesn't pay much, and it surely doesn't have a great retirement plan, but you can't put a price on a caring mom who invests in her family. Your daughter needs to know how valuable—how incredibly priceless and rewarding—such an investment is.

One last point before we hit our final slow fact.

A mother is her daughter's primary role model. If she has embraced strong, biblical femininity, she'll give her daughter something to emulate. A warm relationship with her mom is important to a daughter. But if Mom has bought into feminism, you will need to graciously address that. Your wife needs to hear your concern, but she also needs to feel understood and validated by you. Is there a deep wound from a man in her life? Did she grow up without a strong feminine role model? Pray for wisdom to know how to approach your wife about this and win her over. It will take time, and you will need to do a lot of listening, but it will be worth it.

SLOW FACT #2: BIBLICAL FEMININE SEXUALITY IS UNDER ASSAULT

Caution is needed as we approach this next curve. Over the past decade, a multitude of daughters have veered off the road here on their way to becoming women: when feminism is unrestrained, there is a strong lure toward lesbianism.

Feminism's denial of binary (male and female) identity has opened the floodgates to a world of gender confusion on levels that boggle the mind. But for our purposes here, we will look only at the appeal of lesbianism and the influences that cause a woman to be sexually and emotionally attracted to other women.

Feminism and lesbianism are the perfect partners. If women don't need men in general, why should they need them for marital and sexual partnership? Feminists have long held that lesbianism is a highly desirable, beautiful alternative for finding romantic connection and intimacy, leaving out men entirely.[9]

I'll be honest with you: lesbianism is an enigma to me. My guess is that's the case for you as well. To gain understanding, I've sought help from some very wise Christian counselors who work with girls who struggle in this area.

Here's the main thing I've learned and that dads need to know. Lesbianism is not just about sex, although sex is part of it. Lesbianism is a heart issue. It tells girls that their deep need for connection—including sexual connection—can best be met by another woman. *Girls who are drawn into lesbianism have not had their core need for connection and intimacy met.*

Did you catch that? We are back to Fast Fact #1, the core

need of your daughter. Do you see why it's so important that you are there to meet her need for loving connection?

Until the past few decades, very few girls moved into lesbianism. But today it has become very "in," intriguing girls who never would have entertained the idea in the past. Lesbianism's attraction is that it promises to heal wounds and meet their great need for connection and intimacy.

Many factors in a woman's growing-up years can lead her into lesbianism. Often you will find two or more of these together: (1) disillusionment with Christianity; (2) a mother who didn't connect warmly or teach her daughter about womanhood; (3) a distant or ill-informed father; (4) wounds from one or more men along life's path, repelling her from drawing close to other men; (5) indoctrination by teachers and professors; (6) being groomed by a female sexual predator, such as a coach or another influential woman; and (7) extreme loneliness and broken dreams. A young woman with dashed hopes of ever finding a good man to partner with in life can end up in a place of profound depression and hopelessness. And that's where Satan can get a foothold.

There is one more key factor: *personality*. This one is so important that we're going to focus on it in depth over the next few pages. But before we do, let's look closer at what we need to know about the trap of lesbianism.

When disillusionment and confusion grab the heart of a vulnerable woman, it can drive her away from God's good plan and into an unnatural attraction to another woman. Outwardly, the relationship may seem innocent enough. But once sexual boundaries break down, the trap has sprung. "Sexual intimacy" will become interpreted as "love" (as it is in any form of sexual sin), and she will soon find herself in an immoral relationship that she thinks will soothe her loneliness and make her happy.

At this point, you may be wondering, *How can I possibly counter so many influences?* You can't. But don't let the enemy discourage you! You cannot forget that "greater is He who is in you than he who is in the world" (1 John 4:4). The Lord is able to overcome the pull of the world on a girl's life.

There's something else you cannot forget. Your very presence is a buffer against the ungodly messages around your daughter. Your leadership can protect her. Your close involvement will warm her heart toward men. Your encouragement will provide the assurance she needs in the face of disappointment. By God's grace, you can head Satan off at the pass with some simple but important actions.

You don't have to be perfect; you just have to get some facts under your belt and step into her life. The Lord has placed you in a powerful position when it comes to your daughter's sexuality.

Are you still with me? If so, let's get practical. Who is most at risk for lesbianism, and how can a father make a difference in his daughter's life?

The At-Risk Daughter

Counselors tell me that the key factor in predicting lesbianism is personality type (just as personality type often predicts homosexuality in boys). When parents misunderstand this, they miss the chance to save their daughters from a world of grief.

Just as God gave each girl her feminine DNA, He also put within her a unique personality accompanied by certain tendencies and skills. These God-given proclivities are good. They serve a purpose. You don't want to change your daughter's personality. You want to discover her delicate hardwiring and work with it. When dads do that, they save their girls.

Like boys, girls fall across a spectrum of personality types. And like boys, those personalities tend to fall into three categories. On one end of the spectrum, you've got the girlie girls. At the other end, you've got the tomboy girls. Then you have the girls that fall in between. Of course, these lines aren't hard and fast; girls can range anywhere across the spectrum. But for the sake of discussion, these categories will help us identify your daughter's natural tendencies and wiring.

No matter their specific personality, all girls should be able to grow into the full bloom of womanhood. Every little girl is born with innate female traits that derive from her God-given DNA and design for womanhood. (We'll detail them in a moment.) How these are eventually expressed will partially depend on her personality bent. But by the time she is eleven, your daughter should have what we will call her "woman-card"—that secure identification with her God-given womanliness—firmly in her possession.

Let's unpack this.

First, let's talk about girlie girls. They tend to love shopping and fashion, think about their future Prince Charming, and dream about having a home someday. If allowed to grow up without guidance, they can become consumed with looking sexy and turn into flirts. These girls tend to form girlie clubs that other girls—especially tomboy girls—can't seem to break into. (If your daughter is a girlie girl, don't let her do this.)

Then you have the girl in the middle. She can have a girlie side and a tomboy side. These girls may be good at sports and enjoy watching football but also love fashion, dream about boys, and plan lives that include children. They can have close friends who are both girls and boys. While they enjoy being feminine, some may also be initiative takers, ready to move out and shake up the world. This is all about personality.

True tomboys comprise the lowest percentage across the spectrum. These girls don't tend to care about girlie stuff like tea parties in their younger years or putting on makeup and watching chick flicks as they get older. They much prefer competitive sports and tend toward interests less typical for their gender, like climbing trees and playing Xbox. Dresses may be tolerated, but pants work best. Moms have to especially encourage these girls to care about grooming and self-care.

You may have already guessed that tomboy girls are most at risk for moving into lesbianism later in life. If your daughter is more of a tomboy in her personality, she may try to be like the girlie girls, but she will often feel she simply doesn't fit in. If she doesn't find her bearings in adolescence, she may hit an identity crisis. Because of the times in which we live, the disconnect may become so great that she can fall through the cracks and totally lose her way.

Here's what you need to know about your tomboy girl. She isn't destined to be homosexual any more than her highly sensitive male counterpart is. And she's every bit as much a woman in her DNA as any girlie girl.

However, our current culture is so sexually corrupt that some fool is likely to tell your tomboy that she is gay or, worse yet, that she really is a man in a woman's body. And that, my friend, is criminal.

Tomboys have been around since the beginning of time, and it has been no big deal. These girls are usually strong willed, naturally competitive, very smart, and natural leaders. When the Lord grabs their hearts, He uses these girls to influence people all around them. My wife's own mother was a total tomboy. She was highly intellectual, loved chemistry, and was drawn into the field of medicine. She grew up to influence four generations through her godly feminine womanhood. God uses women across the entire spectrum of personalities to influence the world for good. But today an innocent little girl who has fun shooting baskets or digging for bugs can be assaulted by a destructive, satanic lie.

If your little girl is a tomboy, you've got to get inside her heart and protect her. Not all girls are born with an interest in playing house or dressing up in their mom's high heels. This doesn't mean they are gay. It just means they are on a different end of the broad spectrum of female personality types.

Femininity is not about *interests;* it's about an inner *spirit*. Lesbianism is about detaching from that God-designed spirit, blocking it, and shutting it down. Your tomboy has tremendous potential to become a strong feminine woman, a great mom, and an excellent wife who will make a difference in her world.

Be aware that women's athletics is rampant with lesbianism. The higher up you get, the more lesbians there are. Don't take my word for it; listen to counselors who have worked for years with young women who struggle with lesbianism. They give their advice in an excellent video on understanding gender development in girls: *Why? Understanding Homosexual and Gender Development in Females.*[10]

Let's say your daughter is on a Division 1 softball or basketball team. You can expect almost everyone on that team to identify as gay. If she doesn't, they will use the term "token straight girl" because everyone from the coaches to trainers to players will claim to be gay. An insecure girl who's never had a guy show interest in her and joins the team is going to feel tremendous peer pressure to identify as gay.

Counselors say that it is common for a group of girls to get her intoxicated and hit on her to see if she responds. It's almost unacceptable to be heterosexual in an upper-level women's athletic sport today. In essence, it's a club of lesbians you are pressured to join. The pressure to experiment is tremendous.

That is why you need to look for a Christian college that is strongly committed to the Word of God. In my opinion, that's a much better option than sending your child off to the "University of the Canaanites." Secular higher education of today is not education; it is blatant indoctrination against Christian truth. Why would you pay reprobate professors to brainwash your kids and undo the Christian foundation that you carefully established in their minds and hearts?

So if your daughter excels in sports, you need to think hard about all this. I would urge dads to redirect their girls when they reach the world of upper-level sports, because it's a minefield. You don't want to completely shut down your daughter's interest in sports, but instead look for other areas where she excels and help her move in those directions. But while she is in sports, even in the early years, keep a close eye on her coaches. And when she reaches puberty, talk with her about this potential pressure coming her way.

Dads and Tomboy Daughters

It's a serious mistake to treat your tomboy daughter like the son you never had.

A father needs to handle his daughter with dignity and gentleness that honor her fair sex. Open doors for her. Insist on carrying packages for her. Pull the chair out for her at restaurants. Don't make the mistake of thinking that your strong-willed, aggressive, athletic daughter doesn't need those actions from you. She does. She needs time with you that isn't centered on a soccer match or basketball game.

If you treat your tomboy daughter like a boy rather than the woman she is, *she will attach herself to that image and experience*. She gets her cues from you. You can't afford to shrug that off. A father can fully enjoy playing sports, fishing, hunting, and camping with his daughter. But at the end of the day, *you are not a mirror; you are the "other" in her life*. She may be a lot like you in your personality, but she is still different from you. She's a female!

It may surprise you to learn that even though these girls are tougher on the outside, they are often more sensitive than other girls. A tomboy may not cry or show emotion because she thinks it's a sign of weakness. If she doesn't express her feelings at first, that's okay. Just spend time with her; she will eventually talk. She's going to struggle if she doesn't fit into the girlie club. Don't downplay her struggles; encourage her to talk about them. Hug her and hold her. Welcome her tears. And give her your positive outlook on her future.

Your tomboy *especially* needs your affirmation of her womanhood. What are the traits God placed into your daughter when He created her?

- an instinct for nurturing
- a desire to complement, help, and respond to a good man
- an innate need to be protected and cared for

Notice these traits when they show up, and affirm them! Most important of all, *treat her like a woman.*

She will respond when you are affectionate. Tell her how beautiful she is from the inside out. And talk with her about guys. You can do that better than anyone. When you do this, you are saying she can draw close to guys in the way God intended. You're saying she's lovely. You're stamping the image of "woman" on her heart and giving her that "woman-card" every girl must have.

Moms and Tomboy Daughters

A mom is especially important in a tomboy daughter's life.

If your daughter finds a warm connection with her mom, if her mom is there to understand her and teach her about womanhood, and if her mom walks with her through puberty and boys and the tough years of growing into womanhood, it will make all the difference.

Let me be straight up with you: if your wife won't provide what your daughter needs, you have to ask God to bring a strong feminine woman into your daughter's life.

You want your daughter to grow up feeling confident, strong, smart, *and* feminine. A daughter who becomes secure in her femininity is able to trust and respond to men.

She can enjoy her innate gifts of bearing and nurturing a family. She can feel a deep sense of purpose in this world.

Your daughter is very fortunate to have a father like you in her life. You are the compass that points her to the true north of Jesus Christ and His calling and purpose for her. Remember how Caleb gave his daughter the upper and lower springs (see Joshua 15:19)? When we point our girls toward the Lord Jesus Christ, we introduce them to the One who is the ultimate and only source of living water that gives eternal life.

> Everyone who drinks of this water will be thirsty again, but whoever drinks of the water that I will give him [or her] will never be thirsty again. The water that I will give him will become in him a spring of water welling up to eternal life. (John 4:13–14, ESV)

The Lord Jesus knows how to save the girls. You can count on Him to give you the wisdom you need as you seek to father your daughter well.

10

TELLING YOUR KIDS WHAT YOU DON'T WANT TO TELL THEM

There are some . . . men and women at the age of sixteen,
who have nothing more to learn about the erotic.
—Allan Bloom

The photographer for a national magazine was assigned to get photos of a great forest fire. Smoke at the scene hampered him, and he frantically called his home office to hire a plane. "It will be waiting for you at the airport!" he was assured by his editor.

As soon as he got to the small rural airport, sure enough, a plane was warming up near the runway. He jumped in with his equipment and yelled, "Let's go! Let's go!" The pilot swung the plane into the wind, and soon they were in the air.

"Fly over the north side of the fire," said the photographer, "and make three or four low, level passes."

"Why?" asked the pilot.

"Because I'm going to take pictures!" said the photographer with great exasperation. "I'm a photographer, and photographers take pictures!"

After a long pause the pilot said, "You mean you're not the instructor?"

Okay, that was a joke! But guess what? When it comes to teaching your kids about sex, you *are* the instructor. That's the premise of this chapter. It's your responsibility to teach them the fundamentals of sexuality and how everything "works."

The goal is to begin and maintain an open dialogue with your kids. Young people are talking about sex all the time. On the screen, on social media, and at school, kids will be disproportionately exposed not just to questions of heterosexuality but also to the issues of homosexuality and sexual orientation. Don't make any of these subjects taboo. Talk about them even if you're not ready when they bring the topics up. Ask them questions and attempt to answer theirs. (Also, get some help, like Tom Gilson's book *Critical Conversations: A Christian Parents' Guide to Discussing Homosexuality with Teens.*)

Obviously, you're going to begin this discussion way before the teen years. Randy Alcorn cited a survey of seventy thousand children that found that "on average, sexting began in the fifth grade, pornography consumption began when children turned 8, and pornography addiction began around age 11."[1]

This chapter serves as your certification in teaching your kids so you instruct them confidently and wisely with the

Lord's guidance. That means you will intentionally teach your children God's truth in a culture awash in deception and lies. You will intentionally expose the darkness by teaching them the light of God's Word.

Those two things are really the same thing: two sides of the same coin. On one side is heads and the other is tails. Heads is intentionally teaching God's truth, and tails is exposing the darkness of the satanic lies of our contemporary culture.

As you teach them the truth of God's Word with your words and by your life, you are fighting the battle. And you are functioning as the point man, the spiritual leader of your home.

What does that look like in real life?

Early on, you are going to have to step up and talk with your kids about gender. How early? Earlier than you want to. The reason you must do this is that they will encounter this topic as early as kindergarten or first grade.

A wave of transgender propaganda is seeking out the hearts and minds of young kids through the media and in the schools. You must get to your kids before the enemy gets to them. You must talk to them early and appropriately about basic biblical truth. You must tell them that God made people to be only male or only female.

Baby boys are born with a penis, and baby girls aren't. That's been understood for thousands of years but not now, so you're going to have to talk about it in a normal and natural way in the safe confines of a loving Christian home.

You will also have to teach your children about marriage and that God made marriage for only a man and woman. You don't have to make a big deal out of this. Just talk about it and tell them how great true marriage is and that God invented it.

You will have to talk with them about same-sex attraction. You can't wait for them to come to you asking questions about gay marriage. The culture is doing everything it can to rob children of their innocence. In that case, you need to let them know that some people are confused about God's plan but that His plan is the best plan.

So, what do you say and when do you say it?

Leaders lead, and you are going to have to take the initiative here.

First pray. Ask God for wisdom, and ask Him for an appropriate time that He will providentially set up when it will be normal and natural to have these brief but important interactions with your kids. Ask Him to arrange the teachable moments when your kids are tuned in and when you sense God's favor and wisdom in talking with them. You don't have to force this. Ask the Lord to go ahead of you and set up these necessary conversations.

Later, I will recount for you the sex talk I had with my son. But I need to point out that there will be many small conversations leading up to that talk for you. For instance, your four-year-old might ask, "Daddy, why are those two men across the street holding hands and kissing?"

You could answer, "Son, some people are very confused because they don't know the Lord. We know that God has made dads and moms to love each other and kiss, right?"

"That's right, Daddy."

"Well, when we see people like that, we need to pray that Jesus will help them know the truth."

"Okay, Dad."

And then you go about your business. If your child comes back to it later and asks more questions, you will talk about it some more. The depth of your answers will depend on the child's age and maturity. Two excellent books to help you get the conversation started are *Good Pictures Bad Pictures* and *Good Pictures Bad Pictures Jr.*[2] It is essential, especially in our culture, that children get their information about sex from their parents. The reason it is so essential is that there are quite a few other people who want the job. In his book *Grand Illusions: The Legacy of Planned Parenthood*, George Grant described an interview with a young girl named Catherine who sat through a health class at her school:

> Second period on Tuesdays and Thursdays was her "Health" class. . . . This week, a representative from Planned Parenthood had come to talk about sex, contraception, pregnancy and abortion. . . .
>
> "At first, I couldn't tell where all this was leading," Catherine said. "But then it became *really* obvious. [The woman from Planned Parenthood] started asking us personal questions. *Very* personal questions. Like about our feelings, about sex, and even about—well, about masturbation. It was *so* disgusting. All the boys were kind of giggling but you could tell that even *they* were embarrassed. Then she showed us a film that was extremely explicit."
>
> An unashamedly brash couple fondled each other in preparation for intercourse. At appropriately prurient moments of interest, the camera zoomed in for close-up shots—sweaty body parts rubbing, caressing, kissing, stroking, clasping, petting, and

embracing. At the height of passion, the camera fixed on the woman's hands, trembling with ecstasy, as she tore open a condom package and began to slowly unroll its contents onto her partner. . . .

When the lights came back on, the entire class was visibly shaken. With eyes as wide as saucers, the youngsters sat speechless and amazed. But their guest was entirely unperturbed.

"She began to tell us that everything we had just seen was totally normal and totally good. She said that the couple obviously had a *caring, loving,* and *responsible* relationship—because they took proper precautions against conception and disease."

At that, the speaker passed several packages of condoms around the room—one for each of the girls. She instructed the boys to hold up a finger so that the girls could practice contraceptive application.

Already shell-shocked, the students did as they were told.

Afterwards, several of the girls began quietly sobbing, another ran out of the room and threw up, still another fainted. Mercifully, the class ended just a moment later.

"I have never been more humiliated in my life," Catherine said. "I felt dirty and defiled after seeing the film. But then, when I had to put that thing on Billy's finger—well, that was just awful. It was horrible. It was like I'd been *raped*. Raped in my mind. Raped by my school. Raped by Planned Parenthood. I think I was—that we have all been—betrayed."[3]

I'll give you a moment to recover from what you just read. Can you imagine that such a thing actually happened in a public school in this country? Decades ago, prayer was taken out of our schools, along with Bible reading, and the Ten Commandments cannot be posted in our schools, but when it comes to teaching morality (and that's precisely what sex education is), then suddenly there is an open-door policy to godless influences like Planned Parenthood.

Longtime family values advocate Tom Minnery wrote the following enlightening words: "Across the country, local school districts are mandating abstinence as the basis of sex education. Sensing the trend, Planned Parenthood also offers the concept. But it defines abstinence as 'non-penetration'—everything else is OK."[4]

So Planned Parenthood officially endorses abstinence. But according to them, abstinence is "non-penetration."

Let me get this straight. According to Planned Parenthood, if a teenage boy and girl engage in oral sex, then they can truthfully say they are abstaining. Consider this in light of what that great "theologian" (I'm kidding—he's a comedian) Woody Allen once said about abstinence: "I want to tell you a terrific story about oral contraception. I asked this girl to sleep with me and she said 'No.'"[5]

On the surface, it appears that both Christians and Planned Parenthood agree that abstinence is a good thing. Yet, when you look at the definition, Planned Parenthood has something else in mind entirely. H. W. Shaw is often credited with saying, "I have seen hypocrisy that was so artful it was good judgment to be deceived by it." That describes the situation here to a T.

Let's put the cards on the table. A war is raging for our children, and Planned Parenthood and its philosophical cousins are the enemy. They are trying to rip apart every-thing that is right, moral, godly, and decent. And they are walking into our public schools every day with the intention of undercutting the value system of Christian parents. In recent years, Planned Parenthood has introduced its "Get Real" workbook to middle school students. This curriculum is being used across the country by educators to "educate" seventh graders about how to perform oral and anal sex.[6]

In this chapter, I want to suggest a premise, a policy, and a procedure for teaching our children the truth about sexuality. In light of what our kids are learning in school, in the media, and from their friends, we have no choice but to educate them about the truth of God's gift of sex.

Maybe the thought of talking to your children about sex embarrasses you. Allow me to suggest that although you may feel some embarrassment, there is nothing to be embarrassed about. Dr. Howard Hendricks expressed it this way: "Why should we be ashamed to discuss what God was not ashamed to create?"[7]

You cannot afford *not* to educate your children about sex.

I'm convinced that the reason most people don't educate their children about sex is that *their* parents did not educate *them*. As a result, sexual ignorance is passed from genera-tion to generation. It's time to put a new link in the genera-tional chain. If you teach your kids about sex, they will teach their kids, and their kids will teach theirs, and so on down the line.

I've already stated my premise elsewhere, but let me make it crystal clear. *A man is responsible to teach his children about sex.* As a rule of thumb, fathers should teach their sons, and mothers should teach their daughters. But the father, as head of the family, has a responsibility to make sure that each child is given the proper and correct instruction by the appropriate parent at the right time.

The book of Proverbs fits into a category known as wisdom literature. We tend to forget that Proverbs is a book. Our tendency is to break it up into little pieces and pull out the individual proverbs. But Proverbs, like every other book in the Bible, has a specific author writing with a specific purpose in mind. Solomon's purpose in writing is to dispense wisdom.

One evening I read through Proverbs and circled every reference that specifically mentioned to whom Solomon was writing. In 1:8, he said, "Hear, my son, your father's instruction." In 2:1, he wrote, "My son, if you receive my words . . ." In 3:1, we read, "My son, do not forget my teaching." In chapter 4, he addressed his son specifically three times, and so on throughout the book.

The book of Proverbs is a father's instruction to his son about gaining wisdom for life, covering between fifty and eighty topics (depending on how you categorize the subjects).

I've heard wisdom defined as "skill in everyday living." Sex is one of the main issues covered in the book of Proverbs. As you read the passages about sex, notice that the father is clear and direct and takes the initiative. He describes sexual situations that probably will come up in his son's life, then offers the wisdom needed to handle the situation correctly.

Solomon practiced preventive medicine. He wanted his son to know what steps to take in the event that a tempting circumstance arose. Proverbs 5 serves as an excellent example. I urge you to study it carefully and share its timeless wisdom with your son.

Let's make three quick observations about Solomon's approach. In verses 1–6, he tells his son about the kind of woman that will seek to bring him down. She is smooth with her words and extremely enticing. He warns his son about giving in to the impulse of immediate sexual indulgence. He also describes the true character of such a loose and promiscuous woman—what you see is *not* what you get.

In verses 7–14, he gets even more specific. He tells his son not to get near such a woman. He's to avoid going to her door at all costs. If he avoids her door, she cannot bring him down. Toward the end of this section, he reiterates the consequences of becoming involved in adultery. He reminds his son of the great remorse that will follow the adulterous act. "Son," he says, "think about the consequences of your decision before you get into it. Don't do something stupid on impulse."

In the final section, verses 15–23, Solomon tells his son about the advantages of enjoying a pure sexual relationship in marriage. He tells him up front that he is to enjoy his wife sexually and not to dispense his sexual energy to other women. He also reminds him that God is watching his behavior and will severely discipline him if he violates the marriage covenant.

Proverbs 5 shows us that a father is to talk straight with

his son about the boundaries God has put around His gift of sex. Notice that the father doesn't mince any words. He attempts to prepare his son for what might occur long before it happens. This is precisely what we are to do as leaders of our homes.

If this was important in Solomon's day, how much more so in ours?

If you are a Christian man with children, it is undoubtedly your goal and prayer that they be virgins when they get married. I don't think Planned Parenthood shares that goal. We should do everything we can to encourage our kids to remain sexually pure until they walk into the church to be wed.

In our culture, the worst, most derogatory thing a single man can be called is a virgin. But purity is not derogatory; it's exemplary. Boys do *not* have to sow wild oats. That is a myth. What a boy needs to sow from his earliest years are the seeds that will enable him to enter marriage as a one-woman kind of man. He will take that course, however, only if he has a father who encourages him in that direction.

If you are a one-woman kind of man, you should be equipping your son to enter the marriage covenant with sexual purity and truly be a one-woman kind of man from the first day he is married. There are no guarantees in this fallen world, but that should be your goal.

THE POLICY FOR PARENTAL SEX EDUCATION

The policy is easy to remember: *get to your kids before their peers do!* That's it. The question is, At what age will their peers begin to bring up the issue?

If your child is ten years old and doesn't know the scoop yet, get on the stick, because you've got some work to do! These days a ten-year-old knows more than you might think. Kids have already gotten the information. The only question is, From whom did they get it and how accurate is it?

Let's reiterate the policy: *get to your kids before their peers do!* That means that if you're going to err, err on the side of introducing the subject too early rather than too late. Remember, *we fathers,* not some kids on a playground, are to be the instructors of our children.

Your wife can be a big help here. It may be that you are in tune with your son but not getting any signals that he's ready to talk about sex. That's okay. Maybe it hasn't crossed his mind yet. In my opinion, however, as a boy approaches the age of seven, a father should begin to think about an opportune time to speak with his son about sex. He may not be thinking about it, but I guarantee you that at least one of his friends is. The same approximate guideline can be used for mothers and daughters. In some cases, the discussion may need to happen sooner; in others, a little later. If you ask the Holy Spirit to give you wisdom as to the best time for your child, He will give it to you.

So far we have established the premise and the policy. Now let's talk about the procedure.

THE PROCEDURE FOR PARENTAL SEX EDUCATION

One of his closest friends said that Winston Churchill spent a good part of his life rehearsing impromptu speeches. One day his valet, having shortly before drawn his master's bath, heard Churchill's voice booming out from the bathroom.

The valet stuck his head in to find out if anything was needed. Churchill, immersed in the bathtub, said, "I was not speaking to you, Norman, I was addressing the House of Commons."[8] When a man sits down to talk with his son, he should follow Churchill's example. You want to be impromptu, but you also want to be prepared. Here are some specific thoughts and suggestions on how to do this.

1. Small Questions Deserve Small Answers

I heard about a little boy who approached his father after dinner and asked, "Daddy, where did I come from?" The father nearly choked with surprise but managed to gather himself. Because they were alone in the den, he thought this would be as good a time as any, so he commenced to tell the boy about the sperm, the egg, and all the pertinent information. After about five minutes, he looked at his son's blank stare and asked, "Son, is this making any sense?"

The boy replied, "I guess so, Dad, but Tommy came from Cleveland. Where do we come from?"

Make sure you understand the question before you commence with an answer.

2. Big Questions Deserve Big Answers

Years ago, a conversation began while I was watching the news and my son John, who was around ten at the time, was reading a book. Overhearing the newscaster's story, he said, "Dad, what is AIDS, anyway?" That's what you call a big question. It got a big answer. Up to that point in his life, John did not know about homosexuality. After our discussion, he did know about it. And he was shocked.

When I told him there were men who had sex with other

men, he could not believe his ears. I was sorry he had to hear about it at all. But I wanted him to hear it from me and not someone else. These were the pre-technology days, and neither John nor I had access to Siri or the internet. Instead, John "googled" his dad for that sensitive information—and I'm glad he did.

3. Frank Questions Deserve Frank Answers
Another memory of my son John comes to mind. He came running upstairs and said, "Dad, I've got to ask you a question." I said, "Okay, shoot." He said, "It's private." I said, "Okay," and dropped what I was doing (which was writing the original edition of this book), and John shut the door.

He said, "Dad, if a couple gets married and then gets divorced and then later they decide that it was a mistake to get a divorce and they get married again, would they have sex again?"

I have no idea where that question came from, but it was something John was trying to figure out. He asked me a frank question, and I gave him a frank answer: "Yes." He thought for a second and said, "Okay, thanks, Dad," and went back downstairs to play with his Legos.

Regardless of how well you think you are explaining everything, a boy of that age has not put all the pieces together. It reminds me of a story a friend related to several of us a while back. He has three children and was explaining the facts of life to his seven-year-old son. When he told him that babies come from sexual intercourse and proceeded to explain what that was, his boy got an astonished expression on his face and said, "You mean that you and Mom have done that three times?"

4. Be Casual and Natural

The reason for this is simple. If you're tense and nervous about discussing sex, you're going to make your children tense and nervous. The fact of the matter is, there is nothing to be tense about.

You want to create an environment for your children that makes them feel that the most natural thing in the world is to ask Dad and Mom their questions about sex. So be casual and natural. Be relaxed. Even if you're tense on the inside and you have to chew two or three packs of Tums afterward, don't let on that you're tense. Whatever you do, create an atmosphere where they feel comfortable going to you.

5. Look for Teachable Moments

You never know when a teachable moment is going to show up. When one does, make sure you teach. A teachable moment is a special time or circumstance that ignites an unusual teachability in your child. It is a gift from God.

Evangelist Josh McDowell related a teachable moment that happened with his two oldest children. As the three of them were traveling in the car together, his kids got in an argument. "F—you!" said his son to his daughter.

What would you do in that situation? Here's how McDowell turned that into a teachable moment:

> Sean obviously didn't know what the f-word meant.
> If I had jumped all over him and told him how dirty
> the word was, he would have learned not only that
> the word was bad, but he also would have had a
> negative impression about the sex act itself when he
> learned what it was.

So instead I said, "Son, where did you learn that word?"

"On the school bus," he answered.

"Do you know what it means?" I asked.

"No."

"Can I explain it to you then?" I said.

"Yeah!" he answered. "What is it?" He was dying to know. And for the next forty minutes, I had a fabulous opportunity to teach my son and daughter about the sanctity, beauty, and purpose of sex. . . . It was an opportunity for which I was extremely grateful, an experience I'll never forget—nor, I suspect, will they.[9]

6. Use the Right Terms Without Embarrassment

Sometimes this is tough to do. It's not that you will be embarrassed for using the right terms but that your kids will embarrass you when they know the right terms.

Some friends of ours, who are very good parents, have been careful to use the right terminology with their children. One day while grocery shopping, the mother walked thirty or forty feet away from the cart, past the crowds of people, looking for a specific item. Suddenly her three-year-old, sitting in the cart, yelled out with great excitement, "Hey, Mom, look! I've got an erection!"

Sometimes it's tough when your kids know the right terms. But the thing about kids is that they can embarrass you even when they don't know them. So go ahead and tell them the correct ones. You may have to change grocery stores, but that's okay.

7. *Consider the Age of the Child*

We have already touched on this issue, but to underscore my previous remarks, remember that you'll give a five-year-old a different answer to a certain question than you will give a nine-year-old.

8. *Let Your Kids Know They Can Ask You Anything and Get a Straight Answer*

This is the cardinal doctrine of parental sex education. If you establish this, it doesn't matter what they hear somewhere else, for they will come to you for clarification. At certain points you may have to swallow hard before you answer, but whatever you do, don't skirt the issue. Deal with it head-on. This kind of honest dialogue will be the greatest investment you will ever make. It will pay dividends in your relationships for the rest of your lives.

A PERSONAL EXPERIENCE

If you are clued in to the eight principles above, you will create an environment where it is natural for your kids to talk with you about sex. But perhaps until now it's been a closed issue in your home. In reading this chapter and realizing the ages of your children, perhaps you're concluding that it's time for you to do some educating. What do you say now and how do you say it?

First, let me assure you that I'm certainly no expert. Even so, there may be some value in my relating the essence of a conversation I had with John when he was seven. For several months, I had been thinking about having this discussion. I had been monitoring his dialogue with his friends, and I concluded that we needed to talk if I was going to get to my son before his peers did.

John and I had a private conversation one night after dinner. Because it was confidential, I went to him later and asked him if it would be okay for me to relate to others some of our talk that evening. He thought it would be a good idea.

"You know, Dad," he said, "it might help some kids learn about sex and keep them from getting into trouble. If dads would tell their kids about it, it would mean a lot to their kids." So I offer what follows not as a how-to but as a reference that might be helpful as you think through your own "impromptu" talk with your child.

John and I had spoken informally about sex before. He would ask a small question, and I would give him a small answer. But John had just turned seven, and things were changing in his world. After dinner one evening, I decided it was time. We went up to his room and I said, "John, have you ever wondered how God makes babies?"

"Yeah, Dad, I have," he said.

"Well, John, I want to talk with you about that because that is a very special thing God invented. I'm going to tell you some things tonight that you are not going to believe. But before I tell you about this, I want you to understand that it is a great thing and that God created it. It's something He has given to dads and moms that is very, very good. I want to tell you about God's gift of sex. What do you know about sex, John?"

Several weeks earlier, he had told me about a junior high girl down the street who had "sexed." It was clear at that point he had no clue what that meant. But it told me that the subject was beginning to be a matter of discussion. "I know that girl down the street sexed with some boys," John said.

I said, "John, it is very important for you to understand that God has said sex is something for moms and dads only. God says that we are to have sex only when we are married. But some people who aren't married still have sex."

"Really?"

"Yes, they really do. And they shouldn't, because they are misusing the gift God has given, and that isn't right. People disobey God when they have sex and are not married to each other. But God is pleased when mommies and daddies have sex, because they are married."

I started this way because I wanted to lay a foundation. I wanted John to know that sex came from God. I also wanted him to know that sex was a gift from God but that He was very clear about how we were to enjoy His gift. This prevented John from getting the idea that sex was wrong or dirty.

Then it was time to go for it. I said, "Now, John, here is the part that is so wild you aren't going to believe it. But it's true. Let me tell you how this works. When a husband and wife have sex, you know what they do? They take all their clothes off. They get completely naked. And then they get in bed.

"This is when something happens to the daddy's penis. It gets real strong and big. That's called an erection."

Then I said, "John, do you know little girls don't have a penis? Well, they have what is called a vagina. And that's how God made girls. Boys have a penis, and girls have a vagina. When a mommy and daddy have sex, the daddy puts his erect penis inside the mommy's vagina."

I should mention at this point that the eyes were as big as

silver dollars, and the face expressed complete unbelief. (I don't mean John's face; I mean my own. I couldn't believe I was telling this to a seven-year-old!)

"John, can you believe that? Isn't that wild?"

"That's unbelievable, Dad!"

Then I said, "What happens is that this stuff called semen comes out of the daddy's penis and goes into the mommy's vagina. The daddy's semen has inside of it little things called sperm. There are millions of them. They are so small you can't see them without a microscope. Inside the mommy are all these little eggs, which are almost as small. And when a sperm finds an egg and they come together, that's what God uses to make a baby."

I was trying to simplify this as much as possible so that he could get a basic idea of what was happening. You want to use the correct terms, but you want to make your explanation as simple as possible.

"Now, John," I continued, "I know that is really hard to understand right now, but I want you to know that it is really neat. Moms and dads really enjoy that, and you will enjoy it with your wife. But remember, this is something so special that God wants mommies and daddies to do it with only each other.

"John, as you grow up, you are going to have friends and guys in school say things to you about sex. Most of them don't know what they're talking about. The reason they don't know what they're talking about is that they haven't heard about it from their dads. I'm telling you stuff tonight that most seven-year-olds don't know. In fact, you now know more about this than most of your friends do.

"But I want you to understand something very important. If you hear something that you're not sure of or if you have any questions, and I mean *any,* you can come to me and I will tell you the truth. You don't have to be embarrassed, because we can talk about anything. You don't need to ask your friends, because they don't know. But if you come to me, I'll tell you the truth."

I wanted him to know that we have an open-door policy. Believe me, through the years, he used that open door, and I was very glad he did.

At that time, thirtysomething years ago, when pornography was much simpler and pretty much limited to magazines and a few X-rated movies, we also went on to speak about *Playboy* magazine. If this conversation were taking place today, I'd be discussing the danger of sexting and phones instead of *Playboy,* but you get what I'm saying and can work the tech stuff into your conversation as appropriate.

I said, "John, what do you know about *Playboy* magazine?"

"Joey [not his real name] down the street told me that his dad subscribes to *Playboy.*"

"Have you ever seen it?"

"No, but Joey told me that it has pictures of naked ladies in it."

"John, someday one of your friends is going to want to show you a magazine like that. If you see a picture of a naked lady, you're going to like it. But not everything that is appealing to us is good for us. There are all kinds of magazines that show all kinds of naked ladies doing all kinds of things. That's what is called pornography.

"And even though it's tempting to look at those magazines, it's very important that you don't. It's very important, John, that you protect your mind. Let me ask you a question, and it's kind of a gross situation. If you were thirsty and you went to get a drink of water and for some reason the water wouldn't come out of the tap, would you walk over to the toilet and scoop some water out and drink it?"

"Dad, that's gross! I would never do that."

"I know you wouldn't, John, but that's what you do to your mind when you look at pornography. It's like putting toilet water in your mind. And you want to protect your mind. So when someone wants you to look at that stuff, be man enough to walk away. They'll probably make fun of you. But you tell them that you're not going to drink toilet water. You're smarter than that."

What I was doing here was attempting to instill in John the principle of standing alone. I wanted my child to be strong enough to stand against the current of peer pressure. So I painted a probable situation, described how he should respond, described how others would respond, and then gave him something to say so that he would be prepared.

"John, some of the ladies in those pictures have very sad lives. Most of them come from homes where their dads didn't love them, and they're trying to get attention. Some of those ladies are drug addicts and let men take pictures of them naked so they can get money to buy drugs. But you know what, John? We ought to feel sorry for those ladies. They don't know Jesus, and most of them have terrible family situations, if they even have a family. But every one of them is somebody's daughter or sister or mommy."

John was horrified that someone's mom or sister or daughter would do such a thing. When I put pornography in the context of family relationships, it put a different light on it for him. He also felt bad that some women would act like that to get money for drugs.

I was trying here, in advance, to give him a perspective on

pornography before he came across it. I was trying to give him a viewpoint on pornography that would offset its initial allure. Granted, the whole issue has been greatly complicated in today's world with the easy access to digital porn. Nevertheless, it's still critical for a dad to sit down with his young son and explain the dangers out there in cyberspace before he falls into them.

I'm glad I got to John before his peers did. Inevitably, when you have a talk like that, not only will you answer some questions, but you will also raise others. That's why I emphasized the fact that he could ask me anything and I would give him a straight answer.

A few weeks later, we were shooting baskets after dinner and he said, "Dad, I need to ask you a question." He had been thinking about some things, and we casually talked as we practiced our bank shots.

A couple more weeks went by and he asked my wife about the eggs inside a mommy. He couldn't figure out what would happen if those eggs cracked inside her. Now, his question made a lot of sense to me when I heard it. The only eggs John had ever seen were the ones in the refrigerator. Mary explained to him the difference. I was glad he felt that he could approach his mom to ask her a question about girls. In a healthy home, at various times there will be appropriate input from mother to son, and father to daughter.

I would say that for the next year or so after we had our talk, John asked me a question about sex every week or two. It was as natural for him to ask me about sex as it was to talk about football. That's the way it should be. For example, one time we were coming home from running some errands, and as we were getting out of the car, John asked, "Dad, is sex fun?"

I said, "John, you can't believe how much fun it is." That was the extent of the conversation. We then walked into the house and unloaded the groceries.

Now John had a context to hear those words. He knew there are rules for sex that make it fun, just like there are rules for football that make it fun. If the other team gets five downs, that's no fun. Our kids need to hear from us that sex is positive, fun, and enjoyable within the boundaries God has set.

The key word in all this discussion about sex is not *rules*—it is *relationship*. Our children should know that there are rules, but they should learn about them only from the context of a relationship that is open, warm, and loving.

GO FOR IT!

Good luck on preparing your impromptu talk. God will give you the wisdom you don't have. If you don't know the answer to your son's question, say, "I don't know, but I'll find out and get back to you." Then find out and get back to him.

Guys, this is our responsibility. Dads teach boys; moms teach girls. I think that's God's way.

Without your help, there is a real chance your kids could become another number on the teen-pregnancy charts or the abortion reports or the latest findings on sexually active teenagers. There are no guarantees, but if you do your job in this area, you will greatly increase the chances of keeping your children from becoming statistics.

11

START YOUR OWN NATION

Even the poorest man that has a family is to be prophet,
priest, and king in his own home.

—*Oliver Heywood*

It was relatively easy to follow Christ in the United States
for the first two-hundred-plus years. But as we have seen,
those days are over.

It used to be that a man who loved the Lord and led his
family was called a "God-fearing man" and that was a compliment. Today, if you're called a God-fearing man, it's
likely you're being mocked. That's what happens when a nation dies spiritually and falls apart.

But that doesn't mean we lose hope and dread the future.
It just means we have our work cut out for us.

You wouldn't have read this far if you didn't want to follow Christ and be the point man for your family. So what do

you do when the nation continues to pursue darkness instead of the Light?

If the nation you live in is falling apart, *then start your own nation.*

Every nation began with a family, and the nation starts with a man. The book of Acts says of God, "He made from one man every nation of mankind to live on all the face of the earth, having determined their appointed times and the boundaries of their habitation" (17:26).

Think about it. Somewhere back in history, every nation began with one family. And because we have in the Bible a true record of world events, we can actually pinpoint that "somewhere." It's described in Genesis 7:1, when the Lord told Noah to take his entire family—including his wife, his three sons (Shem, Ham, and Japheth) and their wives—and get into the ark. For the very first time, rain fell on the earth, and it kept coming over the entire earth for forty days and forty nights. The floods covered all the high mountains of the earth, and when the waters finally receded and "the Ark grounded, there were eight people alive in the world, and no more."[1]

When the culture surrounding Noah became hopelessly corrupt and evil, the Lord put him and his family into the ark to save them from judgment. They were the only righteous family on the face of the earth. In our times, in our evil days, things are getting bad. One day they will get as bad as it was in the days of Noah. Jesus Himself told us that "the coming of the Son of Man will be just like the days of Noah" (Matthew 24:37). We may not be quite there yet, but we're sliding fast in that direction.

Every nation starts with a man who finds a woman and marries her.

I know of a man (I'll call him Brent) who was raised in not only a dysfunctional family but a destructive family. His family was hell on earth because of the physical and sexual abuse handed down through several generations. His father was the latest edition of that abuse, and evil beyond imagination was practiced in his home. Brent's siblings were destroyed emotionally. Some were even driven to take their own lives. Brent somehow managed to survive those circumstances and graduate from high school, but he was a bitter young man, full of rage and wanting nothing more than to get revenge on his father.

And then he experienced a head-on collision with the Lord Jesus Christ. When that occurred, Brent's plans for revenge were totaled, and all the bitterness drained from him. The Lord Jesus captured him, saved him from his sin, gave him a new heart, and within a couple of years brought along a godly young woman to be his wife. She, too, had come from a destructive home, and neither of them wanted that for their kids. They were committed to the Lord Jesus and to each other.

This story was happening in the sixties, and America was starting to die spiritually as it abandoned the Lord and the Scriptures. But this young couple decided to seek the Lord. They both might have been raised in living hells, but in their home, in their new nation, they decided to ask Jesus to be the King and to make the Bible their constitution.

Decades later, their children are grown and walking with the Lord. Their kids did not grow up with alcoholic rages and abuse but rather with the attention, affection, and affirmation of a loving dad and mom. These children were raised in an infinitely superior nation.

How can this be done?

You start your own nation by realizing that God has *already* put you into a new nation. The moment that you turn from your sin and call upon the Lord Jesus to save you from it, your citizenship is immediately transferred from the kingdom of darkness to the kingdom of God. Scripture reminds us of that:

> You are a chosen race, a royal priesthood, a holy nation, a people for God's own possession, so that you may proclaim the excellencies of Him who has called you out of darkness into His marvelous light; for you once were not a people, but now you are the people of God; you had not received mercy, but now you have received mercy. (1 Peter 2:9–10)

And again:

> You are no longer strangers and aliens, but you are fellow citizens with the saints, and are of God's household, having been built on the foundation of the apostles and prophets, Christ Jesus Himself being the corner stone. (Ephesians 2:19–20)

Make no mistake; we are still citizens of our countries. That is what it says on our driver's licenses and passports and tax forms. *But we are also aliens.* We are citizens of our countries either by birth or by naturalization, but we can never forget that our true and lasting citizenship is in heaven.

You're to be in the world but not of the world.

You're to be *in* the United States but not *of* the idolatry in the United States.

So as the nation and culture around you continue to erode and fall apart, you can start your own nation, letting that new identity shape your life and your days. The most important thing a Christian man can do in his lifetime is strive to raise a godly family. That's what it means to start your own nation.

In your new nation, Jesus is the King and the Bible is the constitution. This new nation comes into being when a man utters from his heart the same words as Joshua: "As for me and my house, we will serve the LORD" (Joshua 24:15).

YOUR SPHERE OF INFLUENCE

The apostle Paul tells us that every man has a sphere of influence (see 2 Corinthians 10:13–15). You have a sphere, an orbit, of geographical boundaries where you live your life. You live in a zip code, and in the morning—if you're not working from home—you may drive to work in another zip code. You may go to church in even another zip code. For work or a vacation, sometimes you may travel outside your sphere to another state or another country. But you always come home to your sphere.

Inside that sphere are *people*. People you know and care about. People you love and who love you. Your wife, kids, friends, grandparents, cousins, boss, coworkers, and others.

That's your sphere of influence.

That sphere begins with your family. That's your central work and your primary place of nation building. It may be just you and your wife and your kids, but how big will your nation be in a hundred years, when you're with the Lord? Because you are following the Lord Jesus and are a citizen of His kingdom, your most important work is to fulfill the Great Commission (see Matthew 28:18–20). The heart of the Great Commission is to "make disciples" (verse 19). A disciple is a Christ follower.

That starts with your nation, your sphere, and your influence.

And where does it end? Only God knows.

Jesus once told His disciples, "You are the light of the world—like a city on a hilltop that cannot be hidden" (Matthew 5:14, NLT). If you have really launched a new nation with Jesus as King and God's Word as your guide, road map, and constitution, and if you have raised the banner of heaven up your family flagpole, you won't be able to hide. You're an alien. Your neighbors and coworkers will see it. People moving by you in the dark, people you don't know and may never even meet, will see the lights of your city-state and wonder at it.

There is no way to measure the impact of a strong, happy Christian family on our dark and disillusioned contemporary culture.

And it all begins with one man.

You.

Your leadership is critical when the culture around you is crumbling.

Quite frankly, I don't have what it takes to lead my family in these troubled times, and neither do you. Apart from the Lord we can do nothing. But with Him we can do anything that is demanded of us—no matter what times we're living in. The Lord knows what a man needs in order to lead his family in the twenty-first century. It was the philosopher Georg Hegel who said, "We learn from history that we do not learn from history."[2] Well, this is a lesson that we need to learn because it's essentially a game plan on how to deal with what is coming straight at us. In fact, those of us who are leading our families need to be aware of a history lesson that is almost 2,700 years old.

The Lord knew what the people of Judah needed back in 597 BC, when they found themselves held captive in the foreign capital of Babylon. The nation of Judah had fallen apart, but that had not taken the Lord by surprise. He knew when it would happen down to the minute, and He had instructions printed out and ready to go for His people who were grieving the loss of the nation and dreading the coming change.

Actually, the Lord has given His people clear directions in Scripture on how to live in *any* nation and culture that is in rebellion toward the Lord. That's where we are now in the 2020s, so we should probably listen up.

THE BABYLON DIRECTIVE

In the Old Testament era, the Lord sent the nation of Judah into captivity in Babylon for seventy years. The people of God were being disciplined by the Lord for their centuries of idolatry, brutality, child sacrifice, and sexual immorality that was a part of idol worship. Even the true believers, like Daniel and his three friends, had to take the long march to captivity in Babylon.

The people lost their country, their king, their liberty,

their land, and their free-enterprise system. Philip Ryken described their dilemma:

> What should God's people do when their zip code places them in Satan's precincts? When God's people were captives in Babylon, they might have expected God to tell them to run away. Or revolt. *What he did instead was tell them to make themselves at home. The gist of Jeremiah's prophecy was that God was going to build his city in the middle of Satan's city.*[3]

To put it another way, the Lord gave clear instructions to the men of Judah to build their little nations and keep on living normal lives. Here's what He told the exiles via the prophet Jeremiah:

> Build houses and live in them; plant gardens and eat their produce. Take wives and have sons and daughters; take wives for your sons, and give your daughters in marriage, that they may bear sons and daughters; multiply there, and do not decrease. But seek the welfare of the city where I have sent you into exile, and pray to the LORD on its behalf, for in its welfare you will find your welfare. (Jeremiah 29:5–7, ESV)

In a godless, foreign nation, each man was to follow the Lord and build his own nation by obeying the clear directions of the Lord. And we are to do the same thing in our times. Here are the orders from the King of kings:

- *Build houses.* In other words, go ahead and dig in for the long haul. They could build from scratch or buy a fixer-upper and remodel. That was their call—whatever made the best sense for their family economically. People who are panicked and scared don't build, but God wanted His people to demonstrate their trust in Him by putting down deep roots.
- *Plant gardens and eat the produce.* In other words, start a small business. They fed their families by farming their little plots and sold the rest of the vegetables at the market to pay the mortgage. Provide for your family. Don't be driven by fear. Ask God for wisdom, use your skills and gifts, and get to work to pay the bills. If you get canceled and lose your job, can the Lord provide another? What do you think? Is anything too hard for the Lord? He makes a way where there is no way.
- *Get married and start a family.* Don't be thinking that things are too uncertain and the future too bleak for you to get married. Find a godly woman, marry her, and start rolling out those kids. It's a Psalm 127 and 128 thing.
- *Prepare your sons and daughters to get married.* If you're twenty or thirty years further down the road with a wife and children, you just keep living life. When you see a young man who you think would be a good match for your daughter, have him fill out an application. Obviously, I am kidding. But next to following Christ, the choice of a mate is the most important decision your children will make. And while you're preparing your kids for marriage, prepare

them so that they will look forward to having children and raising up the next generation. (By the way, this will also give you some grandkids to hang out with.)

- *Don't decrease the population of your nation.* God says to keep increasing your family and your nation. So do it. "Family planning" means planning to have a family. And a substantial one, if possible.
- *Be a good citizen.* Remember how Mordecai, in the book of Esther, uncovered an assassination plot against the king of Persia and reported it to the authorities (see Esther 2:21–23)? Be on your toes like him and stay alert. Pay your taxes on time, and don't park twelve old cars in your front yard. Pray for the welfare of the godless community, for in its welfare you will have welfare. Welfare in this context doesn't mean government handouts. Welfare means peace.

Do you see the hope that the Lord gave to the people of Judah, even though they were essentially captives in a nation far from home? He's giving us the same hope. The Lord gives hope, even in the worst of times. And make no mistake; when the Jews were exiled to Babylon, it was the worst situation imaginable.

If you scroll down a few verses in Jeremiah 29, you'll find a massive vitamin B-12 shot of hope:

> I know the plans I have for you, declares the Lord, plans for welfare and not for evil, to give you a future and a hope. Then you will call upon me and come and pray to me, and I will hear you. You will seek me and find me, when you seek me with all your heart. (verses 11–13, ESV)

This promise was specifically given to those people living in Babylon, but is it not true that the faithfulness of God extends to all generations? This wasn't a blanket promise that their lives would be easy, but it was an assurance that the Lord was overseeing their circumstances and would honor those who sought Him with all their hearts. He would make a way for them. Even in the toughest of times, He wanted them to keep living as normally as possible and trusting in Him for everything they needed.

How's that for encouragement? In the worst of times, God has a future and a hope for you. In Psalm 138:8, David declares, "The LORD will accomplish what concerns me." And the Lord will do the same for you. But you have to go all in with the Lord Jesus.

As Jeremiah 29:13 tells us, you have to seek Him with a whole heart. Half-hearted won't cut it. If you go all in with Him, then at the right time He will restore your fortunes. I can't tell you how He will do it or when He will do it. But if the Lord says He's going to do it, then just hang on.

He will give you what you need at the exact right moment. That's just what He does. He's a great Savior.

SURROUNDED BUT NOT SUBDUED

At times, God's people find themselves governed and surrounded by the godless.

Any government or nation, when it leaves the principles that God has set down in Scripture, can become a prison. Babylon became a prison for Daniel and the exiles. The nations that fell to the Nazis in World War II became prisons. The United States is becoming more and more a nation of

bureaucracy and endless regulations set by unelected officials and judges, along with tyrannical governors and may-
ors who want to close down churches that preach the gospel
of Jesus Christ. They are the greatest threat to our religious
liberty. Such a culture that ignores the law and constitution
is smothering and claustrophobic, even without wearing a
mask. And when the law is ignored, we look around and
find that—just as the Lord Jesus indicated in Matthew
24:12—lawlessness is increasing. As a result, we have out-
breaks of rioting, looting, and anarchy from sea to shining
sea.

So what do we do?

The short answer is that we do not run and we do not
hide. We stay at our posts and do not abandon them. This
doesn't mean that the Lord couldn't lead a husband and
wife to move their family to another state. Just make sure
your decision is made out of faith and not fear.

The Lord Jesus Christ has not sounded the retreat; He
has instructed us to occupy until He comes (see Luke 19:11–
13). We are to serve Him in our work; love our wives; teach,
nurture, discipline, and love our children; and be a rock for
Christ in our homes and churches. The key is to seek the
Lord and ask for His wisdom:

> The LORD is my light and my salvation;
> Whom shall I fear?
> The LORD is the defense of my life;
> Whom shall I dread?
> When evildoers came upon me to devour my flesh,
> My adversaries and my enemies, they stumbled and fell.
> Though a host encamp against me,
> My heart will not fear;

Though war arise against me,
In spite of this I shall be confident. (Psalm 27:1–3)

As Martyn Lloyd-Jones put it, "Faith is a refusal to panic."[4] God has a plan and He intends to use you in its achievement. It is no accident that you were born in these days or that you are raising children in such a time as this. God has promised to give you the tools and the skill to wage this new kind of battle, and He will fight for you because He is on your side.

I understand that starting a new nation may seem overwhelming. But know this: it can be done, and it will be accomplished one day at a time.

When the nation of Judah went into captivity, the prophet Jeremiah was so grieved that he lost all hope. You can read his personal journal of grief in the book of Lamentations. But even in his lowest moments, when all hope was gone over the death of his nation, he pulled himself together and focused on some facts:

This I call to mind,
    and therefore I have hope:

The steadfast love of the LORD never ceases;
    his mercies never come to an end;
they are new every morning;
    great is your faithfulness. (3:21–23, ESV)

Without those facts, you can't build a new nation. With them, you can't be stopped.

Each morning when I wake up, within ten minutes I recite those verses to myself. I invite you to do so also.

It's a Herculean task to lead a family, but with the power of God supporting you, it is a tremendous privilege. If each of us is willing to become the point man in his family, we can count on God's support and power. He's looking for men who will follow Jesus Christ and burn their ships behind them. When He finds those men, He will take extraordinary measures to buttress, bolster, and carry them along in His limitless strength: "The eyes of the LORD move to and fro throughout the earth that He may strongly support those whose heart is completely His" (2 Chronicles 16:9).

May we be those men! And may He give us the strength to withstand the onslaught of His blessing.

APPENDIX

THE MEANING OF HEADSHIP IN THE NEW TESTAMENT

David Roper is one of my all-time favorite Bible teachers. When I was in seminary, I heard him tell the following story:

> A number of years ago I was with my family at a conference center. Carolyn and I were seated in the lodge, waiting for dinner to be served. Right behind the lodge was an embankment that recently had been seeded. There were signs posted that said, KEEP OFF THE BANK. Two of our sons, who were then quite young, were playing at the top of the embankment.
>
> Suddenly the director of the conference, who was seated with us, jumped to his feet and shouted, "Stay off the bank!" and ran out the door. To my horror, as I looked out the window, there was one of our boys poised right at the top of the bank. The director was shouting, "Get off! Get off the bank!" but down the bank the boy slid, right into his arms. The director shook him. "Son, didn't you hear me say, 'Stay off the bank'?"
>
> Of course, I was mortified. I took my child

around the building, got out a little switch, and worked him over. I kept saying, "Son, didn't you hear the man say, 'Stay off the bank'?" As we were walking back he looked up at me with tear-stained eyes and said, "Daddy, what's a bank?"[1]

That little guy had a rough experience because he didn't understand something that was so obvious to everyone else. Obviously, David felt terrible when he understood the problem. David knew what a bank was, and the conference director knew what it was, but David's little boy didn't have a clue what it was.

There are several possible meanings for the word *bank*. Personally, I have fished off a bank, cashed a check at a bank, spent hours on a basketball court shooting bank shots, and assured someone else that I would keep a promise by saying, "You can bank on it."

Some folks who reject the idea that God has assigned men and women differing roles—that is, those in the "egalitarian" camp—have attempted to show that the Greek word translated *head* should instead be translated *source*. If this is the case, then the husband is not primarily responsible to God for family decisions.

Dr. Wayne House pointed out the textual difficulty for such a view:

> Some feminists go to great lengths to argue that to be one's "head" means to be one's "source." Based on this, the text supposedly teaches that Christ is the source of man, the man is the source of the woman, and God is the source of Christ.
>
> The inescapable problem with this view, however,

is that the meaning for "head" is questionable. There is no clear example of the Greek word for "head" meaning "source" during the times of the writing of the New Testament, nor is any example in the New Testament reasonably translated this way. It is a forced, artificial definition of a New Testament word, adopted to support a predetermined interpretation.[2]

John Piper asked, "What is the meaning of 'head' in Ephesians 5:23? The Greek word 'head' (*kephale*) is used in the Old Testament sometimes to refer to a chief or leader." Piper went on to point out that "Paul's own use of the word 'head' in Ephesians 1:22 unquestionably carries with it the idea of authority."[3]

Headship means that in the marriage relationship, the husband has the God-ordained authority and primary responsibility to lead the family. In contemporary terms, the buck stops with him.

Another scriptural support used by those in the egalitarian or "two-headed" camp is Galatians 3:28: "There is neither Jew nor Greek, slave nor free, male nor female, for you are all one in Christ Jesus" (NIV).

The context of this passage is critically important. The text here is not addressing the marriage relationship or how it is to function. It is not speaking about marriage at all. Some have gone to this passage to argue there is to be no captain or co-captain in the marriage relationship. They claim that this passage implies there are to be two captains in the marriage cockpit. They believe this text erases any differences between husbands and wives, differences that are clearly taught in other portions of the New Testament. The problem with such a conclusion is that the context demonstrates that the verse has nothing to do with the subject of marriage.

None of us appreciate having our remarks taken out of context. I think it's only fair that we extend the same courtesy to Paul for his inspired remarks in Galatians 3:28.

What, then, is Paul saying in this verse? James Hurley wrote,

> Within its context, Galatians 3:28 addresses the question, "Who may become a son of God, and on what basis?" It answers that any person, regardless of race, sex, or civil status, may do so by faith in Christ. . . . The gospel is for all persons.[4]

That was a radical teaching in Paul's day. Some today accuse Paul of trying to diminish the importance or status of women in the church, but nothing could be further from the truth. Just the opposite is true. A popular Jewish prayer was making the rounds during the era of the New Testament. It went like this:

> Blessed art thou, O Lord our God, King of the universe,
> > who hast not made me a heathen [a Gentile].
> Blessed art thou, O Lord our God, King of the universe,
> > who hast not made me a slave.
> Blessed art thou, O Lord, our God, King of the universe,
> > who hast not made me a woman.[5]

The thrust of this prayer was not a hatred or distrust of women. Rather, it reflects the false notion that only a male Jew who was not a slave could be a first-class citizen in the kingdom of God. Galatians 3:28 attacks that conclusion like a pit bull going after a mailman. Paul was refuting the religious discrimination that had crept into the practice of the religious leaders of his day. The apostle loudly declared that the gospel was not just for male Jews who were free; the gospel was, and is, for everyone. That is the point of Galatians 3:28. *Paul was raising the status of women, not diminishing it.*

Aristotle once said, "The female is a female by virtue of a lack of certain qualities. We should regard the female in nature as afflicted with natural defectiveness."

Hundreds of years later, Napoleon was reported to have made the following comment: "Nature intended women to be our slaves. They are our property; we are not theirs. They belong to us, just as a tree that bears fruit belongs to a gardener."

Neither of those statements, of course, even comes close to reflecting the biblical teaching about the role of women. Wherever Christianity has gone throughout the world, the position of women has been elevated and improved.

A Christian man views his wife with tremendous respect, for she, too, is made in the image of God and has access to the very throne room of God. But the husband has been appointed by God as the leader in the marriage relationship. He is the captain of the marriage ship. He will give an account to the Lord for the decisions made in his home, and he forgets or rejects that appointment at his own peril.

QUESTIONS FOR DISCUSSION AND REFLECTION

CHAPTER 1: POINT MAN ON PATROL

1. Why might the husband/father be the key to the healthy life of any family?
2. What would you say are the major threats to your marriage?
3. What are the major threats to your family as a whole?
4. Steve told of the two strategies Satan uses in his war on the family: first, *to effectively alienate and sever a husband's relationship with his wife,* and second, *to effectively alienate and sever a father's relationship with his children.*

   What evidence have you seen of these strategies in your family? What have you done to combat them?
5. In what ways can you build your family on the rock—the truths of Scripture?

CHAPTER 2: SAVE THE BOYS

1. Steve wrote that the enemy—Satan—has one simple goal: *destroy the boys by neutralizing the fathers.* What are some tactics the enemy uses to neutralize a father?

2. Does your line of work help or hurt your efforts to be there for your son(s)? Explain your answer. If it's hurting your efforts, list some ways you could increase opportunities to be there for your boy(s).
3. Do you agree or disagree with Steve's contention that men today have been feminized? What are the reasons for your answer?
4. What qualities define a strong Christian man? A strong husband? A strong father?
5. What personal strengths, abilities, and interests of your son(s) do you want to better encourage and support in the future?

CHAPTER 3: REAL MEN DON'T

1. Do you agree or disagree that morality in America has declined in recent decades? Elaborate on your answer.
2. What are the dangers of emotional distance between a husband and wife?
3. In what situations are you more vulnerable to the temptation to be unfaithful to your wife?
4. How would you describe an emotional affair?
5. What can you do to guard against having an affair?

CHAPTER 4: A ONE-WOMAN KIND OF MAN

1. In the context of marriage, what does it mean to "burn your ships"?
2. What qualities would you list that define a "one-woman kind of man"?

3. Be honest with yourself—in what ways do you struggle to honor your commitment of faithfulness to your wife? How might you best guard against failing in these areas?
4. Why are transparency and honesty so important in marriage?
5. If you're struggling with sexual sin, who might offer you wisdom and help? Contact that person today!

CHAPTER 5: ANOREXIC MEN AND THEIR BULIMIC COUSINS

1. If you are going to lead your family well, why is it so important to be a "spiritual self-starter"? What are the qualities of a spiritual self-starter?
2. Why does Satan work so hard to keep us from knowing and applying the truths of the Bible?
3. Why is the discipline of daily Scripture reading so important?
4. Steve wrote, "The danger comes when I listen to a sermon or go to a Christian seminar or listen to a podcast without applying the truth I hear to my life. That is spiritual bulimia." Have you ever struggled with spiritual bulimia? What would be the cure?
5. What steps might you take to better fill your mind and heart—and actions—with the truth of God's Word? Psalm 1:3 describes the results process as "he will be like a tree firmly planted by streams of water." What does that look like in tangible terms?

CHAPTER 6: HUSBAND AND WIFE TEAMWORK IN THE MARRIAGE COCKPIT

1. Based on your experience, why is it so important for you and your wife to be a team?
2. How would you define mutual accountability in marriage? Mutual submission in marriage?
3. What are the differences between a husband who has "authority" and one who demonstrates "authoritarianism"?
4. How does a man's passivity in marriage and the family bring harm?
5. In what areas do you need to become more of a "just as" mature man in your marriage? (By way of reminder, Ephesians 5:25 says, "Husbands, love your wives, *just as* Christ loved the church and gave Himself up for her.")

CHAPTER 7: RESTORING THE ANCIENT BOUNDARIES OF GENDER AND MARRIAGE

1. Why is an attack against traditional gender boundaries an attack on the image of God?
2. Steve wrote, "In our culture right now, two things are being assumed and they both are lies from the enemy. First, *gender is not fixed; it is fluid.* Second, *marriage is not restricted to one man and one woman.*" In what ways or situations have you encountered these lies?
3. If an acquaintance or family member claimed that a person's gender can be changed, how would you offer a response from a biblical perspective?

4. Why is the notion of "gender fluidity" so dangerous to children?

5. Based on what you've learned in this chapter, what are the more important actions you can take to stabilize your child(ren)'s sexual identity?

CHAPTER 8: HOW TO RAISE MASCULINE SONS AND FEMININE DAUGHTERS

1. Steve identified Ephesians 6:4 as the "true north" for a Christian father: "Fathers, do not provoke your children to anger, but bring them up in the discipline and instruction of the Lord." Explain how this verse influences your words and actions as a father.

2. When you were growing up, how did your father apply the wisdom of Ephesians 6:4? Be specific. What aspects of your dad's fathering approach do you want to copy or change as you relate to your child(ren)?

3. Evaluate your own record in implementing what Steve calls the moral landmarks of being a quality dad. (This is not a test but a way to help you identify areas of strength and weakness.)

Rate yourself 1–10, with 1 being really poor and 10 really great.

Fairness _____

Tenderness _____

Firmness _____

"In the . . . Lord" instruction_____

(This refers to spiritual mentoring and care of your child's soul.)

Total: _____ of 40

4. Steve identified three general categories of boys—rough and tumble, rough and tumble/sensitive, and extremely sensitive. Into which group does your son(s) seem to fit? How will this assessment influence the way you relate to him as a dad?

5. Have you discussed the three categories of boys with your wife and gotten her take on them? How will awareness of these categories help guide your parenting?

CHAPTER 9: SAVE THE GIRLS

1. In what ways has your daughter(s) shown that what she really desires from you is intimacy and connection?

2. What does it mean to you that a father should be a provider and protector for his children, especially his girl(s)? Why does this involve more than providing money and "stuff"?

3. Why is it so important that a dad listen to his daughter(s) and spend significant quality time with her?

4. As your daughter(s) matures through different stages of growing up, how will you best protect her?
    Early Childhood:
    Grade School:
    Middle School:
    High School:
    Early Adulthood:
    Maturity:

5. Our culture bombards girls and women with many harmful messages and outright lies. Which lies do you

think are most dangerous? How will you shield your daughter(s) and train her to confront them?

CHAPTER 10: TELLING YOUR KIDS WHAT YOU DON'T WANT TO TELL THEM

1. Why are parents often reluctant to talk with their kids about sex? Do you have similar reservations?
2. How will you prepare to answer questions from your child(ren) about LGBTQ and transgender issues?
3. In your own words, explain why sex in marriage is a gift from God.
4. How will you intentionally protect your child(ren) from bad information about sex? For example, helping them deal with media? Pornography? Inappropriate instruction at school?
5. Have you ever practiced giving a sex talk to your child(ren)? Practice may not make perfect, but practice will certainly lower the anxiety! At what age will your child(ren) be when you begin this instruction?

CHAPTER 11: START YOUR OWN NATION

1. What's your response to Steve's suggestion that, as a Christian father, you should "start your own nation"? Explain your answer.
2. Why is it possible—even if you grew up in a dysfunctional family or without an involved dad—to start and maintain a godly family?

3. Scripture says that as a believer you are a priest. What can your "priesthood" look like in the context of your family?

4. Make a detailed list of your sphere of influence. Review your list and evaluate where you can expand your influence and leadership.

5. Within your most important sphere—your family—how can you increase your influence? Give this question serious prayer. Discuss it with your wife. Make note of the key areas and keep the list where you will give it ongoing attention.

ACKNOWLEDGMENTS

In 1977, I had lunch with Ray Stedman at the Elks Club in Palo Alto, California. Ray had been pastor of Peninsula Bible Church since 1951. I was a twenty-seven-year-old rookie pastor in my first church.

As we were talking, I mentioned my interest in writing. Ray, who had published numerous books, was very encouraging. He had mentored hundreds of young men, and I was about to receive a shocking dose of his profound wisdom. "Steve, let me offer you some advice," he said very kindly. "Don't publish until you're forty." I saw my entire life pass before my eyes. *Thirteen years?* That sounded like an eternity. But in God's good providence, it's precisely what happened. *Point Man* was my first book, and it was first published when I was forty.

I have now passed seventy, and *Point Man* has crossed the thirty-year mark. I remember well sweating over each chapter in our upstairs guest bedroom and wondering if any men would read this book. Thirty years later, I am humbled and thankful for what the Lord has done. The core message of the book is that God has called men to be the spiritual leaders of their families. That has always been true, and it will remain true. It is a core message in the Scriptures. I wrote *Point Man* because many Christian men had been told that they should be the spiritual leaders of their families but weren't real clear on how to do it. Thirty years later, many inside the church are telling men that they *shouldn't* be the spiritual leaders of their homes. It's just another lie from the enemy.

I'm glad to report that, thirty years after the release of *Point Man*, I'm still healthy and so is the book. But with that many miles on the tires, it was time for some maintenance. Over the past couple of years, I've gotten some new shocks and struts, and with this new revised edition, so has *Point Man*.

In the original *Point Man* acknowledgments, I thanked Dr. John Reed, Scott Ford, and David Martin for their support and input from the very beginning. Charlie Boyd, Doug Daily, and the men of Grace Community Church gave me great feedback as I taught this material on Monday nights in the spring of 1989. Don Lewis, Jay Werth, Dennis Eenigenburg, and Jeff Farrar each took time to make astute evaluations of the manuscript.

With this new edition of *Point Man*, I am grateful for the encouragement of John Brandon, Gary Rosberg, Jerry Foster, Carol Spencer, Bev Cline, Stan Sinclair, Walt Heyer, Lance Bozman, John Conger, Ken Sibley, Jeff Scruggs, and John Traver.

On the publishing side at Multnomah, John Van Diest, Larry Libby, Steve Halliday, and Brenda Jose pulled everything together on the original release. On this new revision, Bruce Nygren and Laura Barker, along with an encore by Larry Libby, put all the editing and publishing parts into a seamless package.

If you read the original *Point Man*, you'll notice that I changed the battleground in chapter 1 from Vietnam to Afghanistan. I did this to make it more relevant to a younger generation of readers. In the original *Point Man*, it was my good friend Stu Weber who recounted his Vietnam combat experience with such vivid detail that I felt I had been there with him. In this revised Afghanistan battleground, three additional American warriors and heroes—Breg Hughes, Ryan Fisher, and Derick Hurt—shared their insights as well. I know you join me in thanking all four of these men for their service and sacrifice.

Finally, I closed the original acknowledgments thirty years ago by writing these words: "My wife, Mary, is the Most Valuable Player of this entire project. Come to think of it, she's the MVP of my entire life. Proverbs 31:10 asks the question 'An excellent wife, who can find?' By God's grace, I did." And it's still true today.

NOTES

Chapter 1: Point Man on Patrol

1. Ben Patterson, *Waiting: Finding Hope When God Seems Silent* (Downers Grove, IL: InterVarsity, 1989), 41, emphasis added.

2. James C. Dobson, *Straight Talk to Men: Timeless Principles for Leading Your Family* (Carol Stream, IL: Tyndale Momentum, 2014), 58.

3. Glenn T. Stanton, "What Is the Actual Divorce Rate?," Focus on the Family, November 4, 2015, www.focusonthefamily.com /marriage/what-is-the-actual-divorce-rate.

4. Gretchen Livingston and Deja Thomas, "Why Is the Teen Birth Rate Falling?," Pew Research Center, August 2, 2019, www .pewresearch.org/fact-tank/2016/04/29/why-is-the-teen-birth -rate-falling.

5. David Kinnaman, "The Porn Phenomenon," Barna, February 5, 2016, www.barna.com/the-porn-phenomenon.

6. Maggie Fox, "Suicides in Teen Girls Hit 40-Year High," *NBC News,* August 3, 2017, www.nbcnews.com/health/health-news /suicides-teen-girls-hit-40-year-high-n789351.

7. David R. Johnson, *The Light Behind the Star: God, a Cop, and Today's Families* (Sisters, OR: Questar, 1989), 13. Used by permission.

8. Author's conclusion after reading George Barna, *America at the Crossroads: Explosive Trends Shaping America's Future and What You Can Do About It* (Grand Rapids, MI: Baker, 2016), 178–81.

9. Barna, *America at the Crossroads,* 181.

10. Tom Peters and Nancy Austin, *A Passion for Excellence: The Leadership Difference* (New York: Random House, 1985), 496.

11. E. C. McKenzie, *Mac's Giant Book of Quips and Quotes* (Grand Rapids, MI: Baker, 1980).

12. J. Robert Clinton, *The Making of a Leader: Recognizing the Lessons and Stages of Leadership Development* (Colorado Springs, CO: NavPress, 1988), emphasis added.

13. Jim Gilbert, "Jim Gilbert's Nature Notes: Birds Flying in V-Shaped Formations," *Star Tribune,* October 31, 2013, www .startribune.com/jim-gilbert-s-nature-notes-birds-flying-in-v -shaped-formations/230052811.

Chapter 2: Save the Boys

1. William Raspberry, "Bring Back the Family," *Washington Post,* July 17, 1989, www.washingtonpost.com/archive/opinions/ 1989/07/17/bring-back-the-family/e4e639c1-66e8-4297-aa84 -ac6826b371d2/.

2. Richard John Neuhaus, quoted in Raspberry, "Bring Back the Family."

3. John MacArthur, "Act Like Men," Grace to You, June 21, 2020, www.gty.org/library/sermons-library/81-82/act-like-men.

4. Dave Simmons, "Dad the Family Shepherd" (unpublished notes, Little Rock, Arkansas, 1984), emphasis added.

5. Samuel Osherson, *Finding Our Fathers: The Unfinished Business of Manhood* (New York: Fawcett Columbine, 1986), 6.

6. *The World Book Encyclopedia* (1959), vol. 9, s.v. "Industrial Revolution," 3752.

7. *The World Book Encyclopedia* (1959), vol. 3, s.v. "colonial life in America," 1576.

8. *The World Book Encyclopedia* (1959), vol. 9, s.v. "Industrial Revolution," 3753, emphasis added.

9. Weldon M. Hardenbrook, *Missing from Action: Vanishing Manhood in America* (Nashville: Thomas Nelson, 1987), 11.

10. Marion J. Levy Jr., *Modernization: Latecomers and Survivors* (New York: Basic, 1972), 117–20, emphasis added.

11. Stephen B. Clark, *Man and Woman in Christ: An Examination of the Roles of Men and Women in Light of Scripture and the Social Sciences* (Ann Arbor, MI: Servant, 1980), 636, emphasis added.

12. James Carroll, quoted in Osherson, *Finding Our Fathers*, 30.

13. Lonely, Anywhere, U.S.A., quoted in Ann Landers, "Too Soon, Children Are Grown, the Years Gone," *Chicago Tribune*, June 2, 1988, www.chicagotribune.com/news/ct-xpm-1988-06 -02-8801040158-story.html.

Chapter 3: Real Men Don't

1. Bruce Feirstein, *Real Men Don't Eat Quiche* (New York: Pocket Books, 1982), 14, 60.

2. Feirstein, *Real Men*, 24.

3. Richard Saul Wurman, *Information Anxiety: What to Do When Information Doesn't Tell You What You Need to Know* (New York: Doubleday, 1988), 109.

4. Dennis Rainey, Family Life Conference Notebook (unpublished, 1976), 22.

5. Warren Wiersbe, *The Integrity Crisis: A Blemished Church Struggles with Accountability, Morality, and Lifestyles of Its Leaders and Laity* (Nashville: Oliver Nelson, 1988), 40.

6. Randy Alcorn, "Strategies to Keep from Falling: Practical Steps to Maintain Your Purity and Ministry," *Leadership,* Winter 1988, 44, www.epm.org/resources/1996/Jun/1/strategies-keep-falling -practical-steps-maintain-y/.

7. Alcorn, "Strategies," 45.

8. Pat Conroy, "Anatomy of a Divorce," *Atlanta*, November 1, 1978, www.atlantamagazine.com/great-reads/anatomy-of-a-divorce.

9. Donald Joy, *Unfinished Business: How a Man Can Make Peace with His Past* (Wheaton, IL: Victor, 1989), 159.

10. Robert Farrar Capon, *Between Noon and Three: Romance, Law, and the Outrage of Grace* (Grand Rapids, MI: Eerdmans, 1997), 109–10.

11. Charles R. Swindoll, *Rise and Shine: A Wake-Up Call* (Colorado Springs, CO: Multnomah, 1989), 198.

12. John Walvoord, *The Bible Knowledge Commentary* (Wheaton, IL: Victor, 1985), 468.

13. Charles Haddon Spurgeon, *Lectures to My Students: A Selection from Addresses Delivered to the Students of the Pastors' College, Metropolitan Tabernacle* (New York: Sheldon, 1875), 22, emphasis added.

14. Roger Staubach, 1975 CBS interview by Phyllis George, in Kyle Dalton, "What Was Phyllis George's Net Worth at the Time of Her Death?," Sportscasting, May 17, 2020, www.sportscasting .com/what-was-phyllis-georges-net-worth-at-the-time-of-her -death.

Chapter 4: A One-Woman Kind of Man

1. Burton Hillis, quoted in Laurence J. Peter, *Peter's Quotations: Ideas for Our Time* (New York: HarperCollins, 1977), 425.

2. Based on Fritz Perls, "Gestalt Prayer," Gestalt Theory, https://gestalttheory.com/persons/fritzperls/gestaltprayer.

3. "I Only Have Eyes for You," composed by Harry Warren, lyrics by Al Dubin, 1934.

4. C. S. Lewis, "1954," in *The Collected Letters of C. S. Lewis: Narnia, Cambridge, and Joy*, ed. Walter Hooper, vol. 3, *1950–1963* (New York: HarperCollins, 2007), 439.

5. W. M. Taylor, quoted in Bob Phillips, *Phillips' Book of Great Thoughts and Funny Sayings: A Stupendous Collection of Quotes, Quips, Epigrams, Witticisms, and Humorous Comments. For Personal Enjoyment and Ready Reference* (Wheaton, IL: Tyndale, 1993), 309.

6. Justin Taylor, "The Most Effective Technology on the Planet to Block Pornography," Gospel Coalition, June 14, 2021, www.thegospelcoalition.org/blogs/justin-taylor/the-most-effective-technology-on-the-planet-to-block-pornography.

7. Franklin P. Jones, quoted in Wayne A. Detzler, *New Testament Words in Today's Language* (Wheaton, IL: Victor, 1986), 369.

8. William Makepeace Thackeray, quoted in F. B. Meyer, *Back to Bethel: Separation from Sin and Fellowship with God* (Chicago: Bible Institute Colportage Association, 1901), 55.

9. "Dick Butkus: Hardest Hits," YouTube video, 3:39, posted by "USAR8888," December 30, 2018, www.youtube.com/watch?v=lsWqX2LgXN4.

10. Jim Brown, quoted in Richard J. Brenner, *Pro Football's All-Time All-Star Team* (New York: East End, 1996), 89.

11. Deacon Jones, quoted in James Williamson, "NFL Legends: Dick Butkus," Bleacher Report, May 29, 2009, https://bleacherreport.com/articles/188642-nfl-legends-dick-butkus.

Chapter 5: Anorexic Men and Their Bulimic Cousins

1. "Singer-Songwriter Karen Carpenter Dies: This Day in History, February 04, 1983," History, www.history.com/this-day-in-history/karen-carpenter-dies-of-anorexia.

2. "What Are Eating Disorders?," *Psychology Today*, www.psychologytoday.com/us/basics/eating-disorders.

3. Martyn Lloyd-Jones, "Watchfulness: Volume 7—#4201—Ephesians 6:10–13," MLJ Trust, 15:30, https://mljtrust.org/search/?q=Watchfulness+Ephesians+6%3A10-13.

4. George Gallup, quoted in Jim Berkley and Kevin Miller, "Vital Signs: An Interview with George H. Gallup," *Leadership,* Fall 1987, 15, 19, www.christianitytoday.com/pastors/1987/fall /8714012.html.

5. Samuel Johnson, quoted in Martin H. Manser, *The Westminster Collection of Christian Quotations: Over 6000 Quotations Arranged by Theme* (Louisville, KY: Westminster John Knox, 2001), 86.

6. Raymond E. Vath, *Counseling Those with Eating Disorders* (Waco, TX: Word, 1986), 37.

7. Howard G. Hendricks and William D. Hendricks, *Living by the Book: The Art and Science of Reading the Bible* (Chicago: Moody, 1991, 2007), 24.

8. Derek Kidner, *Psalms 1–72,* Tyndale Old Testament Commentaries (Downers Grove, IL: InterVarsity, 1973), 48.

9. Warren Wiersbe, "Preface to God's Hymnal," *Prayer, Praise, and Promises: A Daily Walk Through the Psalms* (Grand Rapids, MI: Baker, 1992, 2011), 9.

10. *Autobiography of George Müller,* comp. Fred Bergen (London: J. Nisbet, 1906), 152–54, emphasis added.

11. The *Topical Memory System* is available in any Christian bookstore or at www.navpress.com/p/topical-memory-system /9781576839973.

12. James Underwood Crockett, *Trees* (New York: Time Life, 1972), 16.

Chapter 6: Husband and Wife Teamwork in the Marriage Cockpit

1. Excerpted with permission from "Miracle in the Blizzard," by Henry Hurt, *Reader's Digest,* February 1990. © 1990 by the Reader's Digest Assn., Inc., 105.

2. Hurt, "Miracle in the Blizzard," 105.

3. Hurt, "Miracle in the Blizzard," 105.

4. Hurt, "Miracle in the Blizzard," 105.

5. Fritz Rienecker, *A Linguistic Key to the Greek New Testament* (Grand Rapids, MI: Zondervan, 1980).

6. John Piper, *Desiring God: Meditations of a Christian Hedonist* (Colorado Springs, CO: Multnomah, 2011), 218–19.

7. Edmund Burke, quoted in E. A. Bond, ed., *Speeches of the Managers and Counsel . . . in the Trial of Warren Hastings,* vol. 2 (London: Longman, 1859).

8. Warren Bennis, *On Becoming a Leader* (New York: Basic, 2009), 192.

9. Mark Twain, "Letter to Gertrude Natkin," quoted in John Cooley, ed., *Mark Twain's Aquarium: The Samuel Clemens– Angelfish Correspondence, 1905–1910* (Athens, GA: University of Georgia Press, 1991), 16.

10. Daniel O'Connell, quoted in John W. Gardner and Francesca Gardner Reese, eds., *Quotations of Wit and Wisdom* (New York: Norton, 1975), 4.

11. I am indebted to Michelle Coffman for this definition.

12. Gerhard E. Frost, *Blessed Is the Ordinary,* quoted in Charles Swindoll, *The Tale of the Tardy Oxcart, and 1,501 Other Stories* (Nashville: W Publishing, 1998).

13. Carl Spaatz, quoted in W. Stuart Symington, "Symington Remembers," *Air Force Magazine,* July 1, 1984, www .airforcemag.com/article/0784symington.

Chapter 7: Restoring the Ancient Boundaries of Gender and Marriage

1. John Trapp, "Commentary on Micah 3:1," *John Trapp Complete Commentary,* StudyLight.org, www.studylight.org /commentaries/eng/jtc/micah-3.html.

2. Stu Weber, *Four Pillars of a Man's Heart: Bringing Strength into Balance* (Colorado Springs, CO: Multnomah, 1999), 50, 35–36, emphasis added.

3. C. S. Lewis, AZ Quotes, www.azquotes.com/quote/867939.

4. Derek Kidner, *Genesis,* Kidner Classic Commentaries (Downers Grove, IL: InterVarsity, 2019), 56.

5. John Stonestreet and Shane Morris, "Was the Nuclear Family a Mistake? Answering David Brooks," Breakpoint, February 24, 2020, https://breakpoint.org/was-the-nuclear-family-a-mistake.

6. Peter Sprigg, "A Parent's Guide to the Transgender Movement in Education," Family Research Council, 2016, https://downloads.frc.org/EF/EF16I43.pdf, emphasis added.

7. See Leviticus 18:22; 20:13; Deuteronomy 23:17–18; Romans 1:24–28; 13:12–13; 1 Corinthians 6:9–10; Galatians 5:17–21; Ephesians 5:5–6; 1 Timothy 1:8–11.

8. John Stonestreet and Brett Kunkle, *A Practical Guide to Culture: Helping the Next Generation Navigate Today's World* (Colorado Springs, CO: David C Cook, 2017), 191.

9. Martin Duberman, quoted in Stonestreet and Kunkle, *A Practical Guide,* 191.

10. Ryan T. Anderson and Robert P. George, "Decade in Review: Marital Norms Erode," *USA Today,* January 1, 2020, www.usatoday.com/story/opinion/2020/01/01/decade-same-sex-gay-marriage-timeline-transgender-consequences-column/2776564001.

11. Elizabeth Hartney, "What Is Polyamory?," Verywell Mind, May 20, 2020, www.verywellmind.com/what-does-polyamorous-mean-21882.

12. Laura Mize, "Americans See Divorce, Fornication, Gay Relations as More Morally Acceptable Than Wearing Fur: Gallup," Disrn, June 30, 2020, https://disrn.com/news/americans-see-divorce-fornication-gay-relations-as-more-morally-acceptable-than-wearing-fur-gallup.

13. From conversations the author had.

14. Walt Heyer, *Trading My Sorrows: A True Story of Betrayals, Bad Choices, Love, and the Journey Home* (Maitland, FL: Xulon, 2006), 140.

15. Cecilia Dhejne et al., "Long-Term Follow-Up of Transsexual Persons Undergoing Sex Reassignment Surgery: Cohort Study in Sweden," *PLoS One* 6, no. 2 (2011), www.ncbi.nlm.nih.gov /pmc/articles/PMC3043071.

16. Abigail Shrier, *Irreversible Damage: The Transgender Craze Seducing Our Daughters* (Washington, DC: Regnery, 2020), dust jacket.

17. Jamie Dean, "Suffer the Children," *World,* March 28, 2017, https://world.wng.org/2017/03/suffer_the_children.

18. Tony Perkins, "The Secret Life of Wisconsin Kids," Family Research Council, February 20, 2020, www.frc.org /updatearticle/20200220/wisconsin-kids.

19. Paul McHugh, "Transgender Surgery Isn't the Solution," *Wall Street Journal,* May 13, 2016, www.wsj.com/articles/paul -mchugh-transgender-surgery-isnt-the-solution-1402615120; see also Richard P. Fitzgibbons, "Transsexual Attractions and Sexual Reassignment Surgery: Risks and Potential Risks," *Linacre Quarterly* 82, no. 4 (November 2015): 337–50, www .ncbi.nlm.nih.gov/pmc/articles/PMC4771004/.

20. Sharon James, *Gender Ideology: What Do Christians Need to Know?* (Fearn, UK: Christian Focus, 2019).

21. James, *Gender Ideology,* 113.

22. James, *Gender Ideology,* 115.

Chapter 8: How to Raise Masculine Sons and Feminine Daughters

1. *Merriam-Webster,* s.v. "compass," www.merriam-webster.com /dictionary/compass.

2. Fritz Rienecker, *A Linguistic Key to the Greek New Testament* (Grand Rapids, MI: Zondervan, 1980), 540.

3. William Hendriksen, *New Testament Commentary: Exposition of Ephesians* (Grand Rapids, MI: Baker, 1967), 261.

4. Hendriksen, *New Testament Commentary.*

5. Robert Coles, quoted in "Reflections," *Christianity Today,* June 16, 1989, 45, emphasis added.

6. Rienecker, *A Linguistic Key,* 540.

7. Martyn Lloyd-Jones, *Life in the Spirit* (Grand Rapids, MI: Baker, 1973), 297–98.

8. John Stonestreet and Brett Kunkle, *A Practical Guide to Culture: Helping the Next Generation Navigate Today's World* (Colorado Springs, CO: David C Cook, 2017), 217, emphasis added.

9. Frank Pittman, *Man Enough: Fathers, Sons, and the Search for Masculinity* (New York: Putnam, 1993), 114–15.

10. Ricky Chelette, *Why? Understanding Homosexuality and Gender Development in Men,* Living Hope Ministries, https://livehope.org/course/understanding-gender-development-homosexuality-males.

11. Chelette, *Why? Understanding Homosexuality.*

12. William Shakespeare, *The Merchant of Venice,* Act 2, Scene 2.

13. Christopher Yuan, *Holy Sexuality and the Gospel: Sex, Desire, and Relationships Shaped by God's Grand Story* (Colorado Springs, CO: Multnomah, 2018), 36, emphasis added.

14. Arthur Bennett, ed., *The Valley of Vision: A Collection of Puritan Prayers and Devotions* (Carlisle, PA: Banner of Truth Trust, 1975), 324.

Chapter 9: Save the Girls

1. Meg Meeker, *Strong Fathers, Strong Daughters: 10 Secrets Every Father Should Know* (Washington, DC: Regnery, 2015), 8.

2. Bonnie Scasta and Ricky Chelette, *Why? Understanding Homosexuality and Gender Development in Women,* Living Hope Ministries, www.livehope.org/course/understanding -homosexuality-gender-development-women.

3. "Child Sexual Abuse Facts," YWCA, September 2017, www .ywca.org/wp-content/uploads/WWV-CSA-Fact-Sheet-Final.pdf.

4. Meeker, *Strong Fathers,* 28.

5. Meeker, *Strong Fathers,* 59.

6. Pitirim A. Sorokin, quoted in "Sorokin: Prophet of Family Decay," *Family in America* 8, no. 4 (April 1993), 3.

7. Michael Novak, *The Myth of Romantic Love and Other Essays* (New Brunswick, NJ: Transaction, 2013), 18–19, emphasis added.

8. G. K. Chesterton, *What's Wrong with the World* (New York: Dodd, Mead, 1910), 164–65.

9. Sharon James, *Gender Ideology: What Do Christians Need to Know?* (Fearn, UK: Christian Focus, 2019), 24–25.

10. Scasta and Chelette, *Why? Understanding Homosexuality.*

Chapter 10: Telling Your Kids What You Don't Want to Tell Them

1. Randy Alcorn, "Parents: It's Time to Wake Up About Pornography, Sexting, and Your Children," Eternal Perspective Ministries, November 21, 2016, www.epm.org/blog/2016/Nov /21/parents-wake-up-porn-sexting.

2. Kristen A. Jenson, *Good Pictures Bad Pictures: Porn-Proofing Today's Young Kids* (Kennewick, WA: Glen Cove, 2018), and Kristen A. Jenson, *Good Pictures Bad Pictures Jr.: A Simple Plan to Protect Young Minds* (Kennewick, WA: Glen Cove, 2017).

3. George Grant, *Grand Illusions: The Legacy of Planned Parenthood* (Brentwood, TN: Wolgemuth and Hyatt, 1988), 106–8.

4. Tom Minnery, "Why Gays Want Marriage," *Citizen,* July 1989, 3.

5. Woody Allen, Goodreads, www.goodreads.com/quotes/115958 -i-want-to-tell-you-a-terrific-story-about-oral.

6. Andrew Beckwith, "Should Your 12-Year-Old Be Forced to Learn Anal Sex?," *New Boston Post,* July 18, 2017, https:// newbostonpost.com/2017/07/18/should-your-12-year-old-be -forced-to-learn-anal-sex.

7. Howard G. Hendricks and Jeanne W. Hendricks, *Husbands and Wives* (Wheaton, IL: Victor, 1988), 233.

8. Winston Churchill, quoted in John W. Gardner, *On Leadership* (New York: Free Press, 1990), 51.

9. Josh McDowell, *Why True Love Waits: The Definitive Book on How to Help Your Kids Resist Sexual Pressure* (Wheaton, IL: Tyndale, 2002), 384.

Chapter 11: Start Your Own Nation
1. Arthur C. Custance, "An Alternative Faith," *Genesis and Early Man,* vol. 2 (Grand Rapids, MI: Zondervan, 1975), 6, https:// custance.org/Library/Volume2/Part_I/Chapter3.html.

2. Georg Wilhelm Friedrich Hegel, Goodreads, www.goodreads .com/author/quotes/6188.Georg_Wilhelm_Friedrich_Hegel.

3. Philip Graham Ryken, *Jeremiah and Lamentations: From Sorrow to Hope* (Wheaton, IL: Crossway, 2001), 410, emphasis added.

4. Martyn Lloyd-Jones, *Spiritual Depression: Its Causes and Cures* (Grand Rapids, MI: Eerdmans, 1965), 143.

Appendix: The Meaning of Headship in the New Testament
1. David Roper, "Helping a Hurting Marriage," *Discovery Papers* (July 7, 1974), 1.

2. Wayne House, "Caught in the Middle," *Kindred Spirit,* Summer 1989, 12.

3. John Piper, *Desiring God: Meditations of a Christian Hedonist* (Portland, OR: Multnomah, 1986), 179.

4. James B. Hurley, *Man and Woman in Biblical Perspective* (Grand Rapids, MI: Zondervan, 1981), 126.

5. Hurley, *Man and Woman,* 62.

ABOUT THE AUTHOR

STEVE FARRAR (1949–2022) was laser focused on his mission to equip men to be the spiritual leaders of their homes and churches. During his many years of pastoring, speaking, and writing, Steve had his finger on the pulse of men and was known for his candor, his humor, and his commitment to Scripture. He held an earned doctorate from Dallas Theological Seminary and pastored for fifteen years, during which time he became aware of the growing crisis among godly men.

He titled his first book *Point Man* because he believed men were called by God to lead their families through the spiritual war that surrounded them. *Point Man* became an instant bestseller upon its release in 1990, and from that point on, Steve focused his ministry exclusively on men.

A man's man who spoke a man's language, Steve was startlingly honest and surprisingly empathetic. He spoke at more than seven hundred men's conferences and events around the world, reaching thousands of men each year. He wrote more than twenty books, including *Tempered Steel*, *Manna*, and *Finishing Strong*. For the final twenty years of his life, he taught a weekly men's Bible study in Dallas that was attended by several hundred men, with an online reach of thousands worldwide.

To access a treasure trove of his resources and teaching, visit SteveFarrar.com.

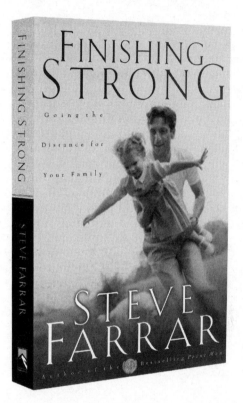